# The Unified
# Process Explained

# The Unified Process Explained

**Kendall Scott**

✦Addison-Wesley

Boston • San Francisco • New York • Toronto • Montreal
London • Munich • Paris • Madrid
Capetown • Sydney • Tokyo • Singapore • Mexico City

Many of the designations used by manufacturers and sellers to distinguish their products are claimed as trademarks. Where those designations appear in this book, and Addison-Wesley was aware of a trademark claim, the designations have been printed with initial capital letters or in all capitals.

The author and publisher have taken care in the preparation of this book, but make no expressed or implied warranty of any kind and assume no responsibility for errors or omissions. No liability is assumed for incidental or consequential damages in connection with or arising out of the use of the information or programs contained herein.

The publisher offers discounts on this book when ordered in quantity for special sales. For more information, please contact:

Pearson Education Corporate Sales Division
201 W. 103rd Street
Indianapolis, IN 46290
(800) 428-5331
corpsales@pearsoned.com

Visit us on the Web at www.aw.com/cseng/

*Library of Congress Cataloging-in-Publication Data*

Scott, Kendall
    The unified process explained / Kendall Scott.
       p.   cm.
    Includes bibliographical references and index.
    ISBN 0-201-74204-7 (alk. paper)
    1. Computer software—Development.   2. Software engineering.   I. Title.
    QA76.76.D47 S35 2002
    005.1—dc21

                                         2001053366

ISBN 0-201-74204-7
Text printed on recycled paper
1 2 3 4 5 6 7 8 9 10–CRS–0504030201
First printing, November 2001

# Contents

# List of Figures

# Preface

## Why This Book?

From the moment the Unified Process made its appearance, I heard many people describing it as really big and complicated, at conferences like UML World and in various public forums, such as Rational's Object Technology User Group (OTUG) mailing list. I agreed that in comparison to other well-known processes, it was rather large, but I didn't think that it was all that complicated, all things considered.

In Chapter 2 of *UML Explained*, I managed to describe the fundamental concepts that underlie the Unified Process in about ten pages. While I was still writing that book, it occurred to me that I could probably describe the most important details of the Unified Process in a book not much bigger than that one (that is, 200 pages rather than my usual 150 or so). So, I set about writing this book partially to debunk the notion that the process contained just too much for the average person to get his or her arms around, and also to establish that the process doesn't specify tasks that people on a project don't do anyway, in one way or another.

The result is a book that I've specifically conceived as a companion piece to *UML Explained*. Rather than try to teach you about the UML, which the Unified Process makes fairly heavy use of, I've included references to chapters and sections in that book that offer details about the various UML diagrams and techniques that come into play within the process. I've also brought a number of the diagrams over from that book into this one, to help the continuity and flow across both books. As Picasso said, "Good artists borrow; great artists steal."

Here are some other key features of this book:

- I've made domain modeling and business modeling, which tend to get short shrift in other books about this process, full players, with the associated artifacts and activities part of the Requirements workflow where they belong.

- I've minimized the amount of project management material. Walker Royce's *Software Project Management: A Unified Framework* (Addison-Wesley, 1998) is the definitive work on how to do project management in conjunction with the Unified Process, and I see no need to try to add value to what he's written.

- Chapters 7 through 9 include the story of how The Internet Bookstore, a sample project, was designed and built. Whereas Chapters 2 through 6 include diagrams from *UML Explained* relevant to that example, the later chapters explain how the project team broke the system down into chunks in the course of doing iterative and incremental development. *Applying Use Case Driven Object Modeling with UML* (Rosenberg and Scott, Addison-Wesley, 2001) contains other views of the same bookstore project. (My attitude is, stick with what you know!)

My goal was to write a book that would demystify what people like to call A Real Big Process or some variation of that. I hope you think I've succeeded.

## Organization of This Book

The body of this book can usefully be divided into four parts.

The first part comprises Chapter 1. This chapter provides an overview of the Unified Process, in the form of a "nutshell" description, some history, exploration of the major themes (use case driven, architecture-centric, and iterative and incremental), and definitions of the major terminology: workflows, phases, iterations and increments, and artifacts, workers, and activities.

The second part comprises Chapters 2 through 6. These chapters provide the details about the five workflows (Requirements, Analysis, Design, Implementation, and Test) that the process defines. Each chapter includes the following:

- An introduction that offers a brief overview of what's included in the workflow and its primary goals

- Descriptions of the various artifacts that get produced during the workflow

- Descriptions of the various roles that people play during the workflow, expressed in terms of "workers"

- Descriptions of the various activities that workers perform during the workflow in order to produce the artifacts

Each of the Activities sections has a diagram that shows the nonlinear nature of the given workflow. Solid lines on this diagram show logical sequences in which to perform the activities; in some cases, one activity is basically a prerequisite to another activity, whereas in other cases, the work that the team performs for one activity will cause a cycling back to one or more activities that it previously performed. Dashed lines are for data flow: The contents of the artifact that results when one activity is finished feed into the next activity or a previous activity.

The third part comprises Chapters 7 through 9. These chapters provide the details about three of the four phases (Inception, Elaboration, and Construction) that the process defines. Each chapter includes the following:

- An introduction that offers a brief overview of what the project team does during the phase, including its primary goals and a high-level look at how each of the five workflows "cuts across" the phase. (You might think of the workflows and the phases as forming a matrix, with the workflows running down the left-hand side and the phases across the top.)

- A description of the tasks that the project manager should perform before the development team begins the activities defined by the phase.

- Descriptions of the activities, defined by one or more of the workflows, that the project team performs during the phase. These descriptions are expressed in terms of what specifically needs to happen during the phase (the team performs an activity to a greater or lesser extent depending on the context) and also in terms of The Internet Bookstore. The bookstore team did one iteration of Inception, three of Elaboration, and two of Construction; each chapter provides part of their story with text that describes what they did for each activity during each iteration and excerpts from the various models that they produced along the way.

Each of these chapters also calls out the deliverables of the given phase at appropriate places.

The fourth part comprises Chapter 10. This chapter describes the Transition phase, which is the phase during which the project team rolls out the system to its customers. The format for this chapter is the same as that for Chapters 7 through 9. This chapter is in a separate part because workflow activities don't cut across Transition the way they do the other three phases, and because the chapter doesn't discuss the bookstore project.

The book also includes the following end matter:

- Appendix A, which describes what the Rational Unified Process (RUP) adds to the core Unified Process
- Appendix B, which compares and contrasts the RUP with the fundamental aspects of eXtreme Programming (XP)
- Appendix C, which describes the ICONIX process, whose roots are the same as those for the Unified Process
- A bibliography, which lists all the books I mention and a few more for the sake of reference
- A glossary, which contains definitions for all the terms I introduce
- A complete index

## Acknowledgments

I'd like to thank another set of Lucky 13 people, while acknowledging that some of them were part of *UML Explained*'s Lucky 13: Ross Venables, for leading the charge to get me the deal for this book; Paul Becker, for always being a supportive and patient editor; Doug Rosenberg, because he'd stop giving me work if I didn't thank him yet again; my reviewers (Jim Conallen, Joel Erickson, Jeffrey Hammond, and Jeff Kantor), for their insightful comments; Daphne Head, just because; Ivar Jacobson, for his encouraging words; Russ Coleman, for not minding that I'm implying that he should be writing his own books; Kim Arney Mulcahy, for helping my books look great; and Samson and Smokey, the dogs who keep me company here in the backwoods.

Kendall Scott
*Harrison, Tennessee*
*kendall@usecasedriven.com*
*http://usecasedriven.com*

# Chapter 1

# Overview

## Introduction

The Unified Process fits the general definition of a process: a set of activities that a team performs to transform a set of customer requirements into a software system. However, the Unified Process is also a generic process framework that people can customize by adding and removing activities based on the particular needs and available resources for a project.

The Rational Unified Process (RUP) is an example of a specialized version of the Unified Process that adds elements to the generic framework; see Appendix A for a discussion of those elements. The discussion in the body of this book about The Internet Bookstore, an example project, represents a tailoring in the other direction: The team doing that project skipped some activities that didn't add value. This example system illustrates a key aspect of how one should put the Unified Process to work: Use those elements of it that add value for a particular project; omit those elements that don't add value. See Appendix C for an example of a streamlined process based on the principle of starting with core elements and adding other elements as necessary.

The Unified Process makes extensive use of the Unified Modeling Language (UML). At the core of the UML is the **model**, which in the context of a software development process is a simplification of reality that helps the project team understand certain aspects of the complexity inherent in software.

The UML was designed to help the participants in software development efforts build models that enable the team to visualize the system, specify the structure and behavior of that system, construct the system, and document the decisions made along the way. Many of the tasks that the Unified Process defines involve using the UML and one or more models.

 See Chapter 1 of *UML Explained* for information about models and their value in software development.

The remaining sections in this chapter describe how the Unified Process evolved, the key tenets that underlie the process (use case driven, architecture-centric, and iterative and incremental), and the vocabulary used to describe the details of the process.

## History

The Unified Process has its roots in the work that Ivar Jacobson did at Ericsson in the late 1960s. Jacobson and his colleagues modeled a very large telecommunications system using layers of "blocks," with the lower layers serving as the foundation for subsystems at the higher layers. (These blocks have parallels with what are now known as components.) The team built those low-level blocks by exploring what they called traffic cases (now called use cases in the UML); all subsequent analysis, design, implementation, and test work was driven, to a greater or lesser extent, by those traffic cases. Other diagrams that are now key aspects of the UML evolved from the Ericsson work, including sequence diagrams (called object interaction diagrams at the time) and activity diagrams (which Ericsson called state transition graphs). A document called the software architecture description contained the key material that facilitated communication among developers and between developers and customers.

Jacobson went out on his own in 1987, starting a company he named Objectory AB. He and his associates spent several years developing Objectory, which was both a process and a product, as is the Rational Unified Process (discussed next). His book *Object-Oriented Software Engineering* (Addison-Wesley, 1995), which described the Objectory process in detail, was regarded as a landmark in the object-oriented (OO) community; it was the first book by a major methodologist to put forth the idea that the customer's requirements, as expressed within use cases, should be the most important driving force in software development. The genesis of the Unified Process's emphasis on architecture (see "Architecture-Centric," on the next page) were also on display in the book. The full on-line version of the process appeared in conjunction with the book in 1995.

Not long after that, Rational bought Objectory AB. Jacobson and his considerably larger set of colleagues set about expanding the areas that the Objectory process didn't address in depth, such as project management and development tools. Grady Booch and Jim Rumbaugh were already on board at Rational— Booch almost from the beginning, and Rumbaugh from late 1994—and the gentlemen who became known as the "three amigos" were among the leaders of the effort to build what eventually became the Rational Objectory Process (ROP), in parallel with their expansion of the Unified Method into what became the Unified Modeling Language.

 See Chapter 1 of *UML Explained* for a brief history of the UML.

While the work on the ROP and UML was going on, Rational was busy acquiring and merging with a number of other companies that made software development tools. These tools added value to the ROP product in the form of requirements management (Requisite's tool became RequisitePro), general-purpose testing (SQA's software has been expanded into several discrete tools), and other areas such as performance testing, configuration management, and change management. In 1998, Rational changed the name of the product to the RUP; the differences between the Unified Process (which is at the conceptual core of the RUP) and the RUP as a product are described in Appendix A.

## Use Case Driven

A **use case** is a sequence of actions, performed by one or more **actors** (people or non-human entities outside of the system) and by the system itself, that produces one or more results of value to one or more of the actors. One of the key aspects of the Unified Process is its use of use cases as a driving force for development. The phrase *use case driven* refers to the fact that the project team uses the use cases to drive all development work, from initial gathering and negotiation of requirements through code. (See "Requirements" later in this chapter for more on this subject.)

Use cases are highly suitable for capturing requirements and for driving analysis, design, and implementation for several reasons.

- Use cases are expressed from the perspective of the system's users, which translates into a higher comfort level for customers, as they can see themselves reflected in the use case text. It's relatively difficult for a customer to see himself or herself in the context of requirements text.

- Use cases are expressed in natural language (English or the native language of the customers). Well-written use cases are also intuitively obvious to the reader.

- Use cases offer a considerably greater ability for everyone to understand the real requirements on the system than typical requirements documents, which tend to contain a lot of ambiguous, redundant, and contradictory text. Ideally, the stakeholders should regard use cases as binding contracts between customers and developers, with all parties agreeing on the system that will be built.

- Use cases offer the ability to achieve a high degree of traceability of requirements into the models that result from ongoing development. By keeping the use cases close by at all times, the development team is always in touch with the customers' requirements.

- Use cases offer a simple way to decompose the requirements into chunks that allow for allocation of work to subteams and also facilitate project management. (See "Use Case Model" in Chapter 2 for information about breaking use cases up into UML packages.) This is *not* the same as functional decomposition, though; see *Use Case Driven Object Modeling with UML* (Rosenberg and Scott, 1999) for an explanation of the difference.

## Architecture-Centric

In the context of software, the term **architecture** has different meanings depending on whom you ask. The definition in *UML Explained* is as follows:

The fundamental organization of the system as a whole. Aspects of an architecture include static elements, dynamic elements, how those elements work together, and the overall architectural style that guides the organization of the system. Architecture also addresses issues such as performance, scalability, reuse, and economic and technological constraints.

Several books offer other useful definitions; see, for example, *Software Architecture in Practice* (Len Bass, Paul Clements, and Rick Kazman; Addison-Wesley, 1998).

The Unified Process specifies that the architecture of the system being built, as the fundamental foundation on which that system will rest, must sit at the heart of the project team's efforts to shape the system, and also that architecture, in conjunction with the use cases, must drive the exploration of all aspects of the system. You might think of the architecture as expressing the common vision that all members of the team must share in order for the resulting system to be suitably robust, flexible, expandable, and cost-effective.

In the context of the process, architecture is primarily specified in terms of views of six models. (See "The Five Workflows" later in this chapter for brief descriptions of these models.) These views reflect the "architecturally significant" elements of those models; taken together, the views form the **architecture description**. The project team initializes the architecture description early, then expands and refines it during virtually all the activities of the project.

The following subsections discuss the key reasons why architecture is so important to the Unified Process.

## Understanding the Big Picture

The tools and techniques available to developers for building software are growing increasingly powerful. For better or worse, though, software itself, especially with its new focus on distributed computing, is getting considerably more complex as well, and there aren't any indications that the tools and techniques will "catch up" any time soon. Also, customers' attention spans are becoming shorter and shorter as their demands on development teams grow more sophisticated. The result is that it's very difficult for all but a few especially gifted people to understand—*really* understand—most software systems to any meaningful extent. The architecture description is meant, first and foremost, to facilitate an understanding of the architecture of the system being built. Rigorous modeling, and careful attention to the readability of the associated UML diagrams and supporting text, will go a long way toward turning the architecture description into the fulcrum for increased understanding of the "big picture" of the new system.

## Organizing the Development Effort

A sound architecture explicitly defines discrete chunks of the system, as well as the interfaces among the various parts of the system. It also makes effective use of one or more architectural patterns, which help shape the development effort on various levels. (Client/server, three-tier, and N-tier are all examples of well-known architectural patterns. Other patterns focus on things like object request brokers [ORBs], which sit at the center of systems that use distributed components, and virtual machines, such as the one on top of which Java runs.) By using this aspect of architecture effectively, the project team can increase the chances that communication across subteams will add value to the effort.

## Facilitating the Possibilities for Reuse

One of the key tenets of component-based development (CBD) is the idea that components should be usable, with a relative minimum of customization, in a variety of contexts. A well-constructed software architecture offers solid "scaffolding" on which components can reside and work gracefully with each other, while making it easy for teams building other systems to identify opportunities for possible reuse of any or all of those components. The bottom line is that the less time a team has to spend focusing on building new components, the more time it can spend on understanding the customers' problems and modeling the solutions.

## Evolving the System

Maintaining and enhancing a system tends to occupy more time over the life of that system than it took to build it in the first place. When development projects find themselves operating in mythical "Internet time," with technologies evolving faster and business models changing more frequently than ever before, there's no question that a system of any size and complexity will be subject to evolutionary changes of a healthy magnitude. Having a solid architecture in place offers a set of essential reference points on which future development work can rely. An architecture that's been built such that changes in one part of the system almost never have adverse effects on other parts of the system also greatly enhances team members' ability to evolve the system effectively and efficiently.

## Guiding the Use Cases

In one sense, use cases drive the architecture of a software system, since the use cases do drive all of the development effort. In another sense, however, the architecture guides the selection and exploration of use cases. Decisions that architects must make about things like middleware, system software, legacy systems, and so forth, have a strong influence on the choice of which use cases the team focuses on at what point in the project. The basic idea, then, is to focus on those use cases that will add value to the architecture, which in turn helps shape the content of those use cases and the nature of the work involved in developing the system from them.

# Iterative and Incremental

The third fundamental tenet of the Unified Process is its *iterative and incremental* nature. An **iteration** is a mini-project that results in a version of the system that will be released internally or externally. This version is supposed to offer incremental improvement over the previous version, which is why the result of an iteration is called an **increment**.

The section "Iterations and Increments," which appears later in this chapter, describes how iterations and increments fit into the larger context of the overall process. Meanwhile, the following subsections describe the advantages of iterative and incremental development.

## Logical Progress Toward a Robust Architecture

An earlier section, "Architecture-Centric," describes the central place of architecture in the Unified Process. The process specifies how the project team should focus on particular aspects of the architecture during each of the iterations of the system. During early iterations, the team puts together a candidate architecture that offers the beginnings of a solid foundation; later iterations find the team expanding the vision of the full architecture, which in turn influences most, and in some cases all, of the development tasks being performed as part of a given iteration. Building the architecture in an iterative and incremental fashion enables the team to make necessary major changes early in the process at considerably less cost than they would inflict later in the project.

## Dealing With Ongoing Changes in Requirements

Processes based on the waterfall approach, which dictates that all of the requirements be gathered and analyzed before design starts, face what now seems to be an inevitable problem: Requirements tend to be unstable. Also, customers have difficulty envisioning a system when all they have is documentation. The Unified Process advocates breaking the system down into **builds**, where each build is a working version of some meaningful chunk of the full system. By focusing on bounded sets of use cases and making effective use of prototypes, the project team and the customers can negotiate requirements on an ongoing basis, thus reducing the (often very large) risk associated with trying to specify all of the requirements up front. One of the reviewers of the manuscript for this book indicated that his company practices "ruthless prioritization," which involves dealing with changing requirements by aggressively identifying priorities and eliminating lower-priority features from consideration.

## Greater Flexibility to Change the Plan

Since each iteration is a mini-project, the project team addresses, to some extent, all the risks associated with the project as a whole each time it builds an increment of the system. As risks become greater, as delays occur, and as the environment becomes more unstable, the team is able to make necessary adjustments on a relatively small scale and propagate those adjustments across the entire project. During the postmortem for each iteration, the project leaders can decide whether the iteration was a success and change the iteration plan as appropriate before work proceeds with the next iteration. The goal is to isolate problems within iterations and deal with them on a relatively small scale, rather than allowing them to spread.

## Continuous Integration

Each increment brings a combination of new features and improved function-ality to the system. This enables all the stakeholders to measure the progress of the project toward specific goals, rather than toward more abstract and gen-eral requirements. By continually integrating new increments, the develop-ment team is also able to isolate problems that it might bring to the system and address those problems in ways that don't disrupt the integrity of the working system. This kind of setup makes it easier for the team to go as far as throwing a particular increment away and starting over, since the process gives it the ability to define iterations that take less time to perform.

## Early Understanding

Each of the activities that the team performs during an iteration is straight-forwardly defined, as is the sequence of activities within each workflow and across workflows. The process is designed to enable reliance on things like ongoing mentoring, rather than forcing people to go through extensive training before becoming productive members of the team. Well-defined iterations allow room to experiment and make mistakes, because those mistakes will be isolated such that their impact on schedule and budget can be minimized. As work proceeds, the team can leverage its understanding of what it's trying to build and the associated risks, thus building momentum, which in turn enables the team to make continuous improvements in the way it goes about its tasks.

## Ongoing Focus on Risk

Perhaps the most important advantage that iterative and incremental develop-ment, as defined by the Unified Process, brings to the table is the project team's ability to focus its efforts on addressing the most critical risks early in the life cycle. The team has a mandate to organize iterations based on address-ing risks on an ongoing basis; the goal is to mitigate risks to the greatest extent possible during each iteration, so each iteration poses fewer risks of less importance than its predecessors.

Various people have come up with many different ways to categorize risks to software development projects. See *UML Distilled* (Martin Fowler with Ken-dall Scott; Addison-Wesley, 1999) for one view of risks. Three categories of risks useful in discussing the Unified Process are described next.

- **Technical risks** are those associated with the various technologies that will come into play during the project and with issues such as performance and the "-ilities" (reliability, scalability, and so forth). For example, if the system will use Enterprise Java Beans (EJBs) in the context of the Common Object Request Broker Architecture (CORBA), the project team must solve a number of potential technical problems along the way to building a system that will perform acceptably. The process doesn't specifically address technical risks; however, the emphasis on architecture (see below) reflects the principle that the team should address technical risks early, before coding starts.

- **Architectural risks** are those associated with the ability of the architecture to serve as a strong foundation of the system and also be sufficiently resilient and adaptable to the addition of features in future releases of the system. Risks associated with "make versus buy" decisions are also part of this category. The process addresses architectural risks by defining activities that involve analyzing, designing, and implementing the architecture, and by defining a number of other activities that include keeping the architecture description up to date so it can assume its place front and center within the development effort.

- **Requirements risk** is the risk of not building the right system—the system that the customers are paying for—by not understanding the requirements and not using associated use cases to drive development. The process addresses requirements risk with activities specifically defined to facilitate the discovery and negotiation of requirements and with its premise that use cases should drive all aspects of development.

## The Four Phases

The life of a software system can be represented as a series of **cycles**. A cycle ends with the release of a version of the system to customers.

Within the Unified Process, each cycle contains four phases. A **phase** is simply the span of time between two **major milestones**, points at which managers make important decisions about whether to proceed with development and, if so, what's required concerning project scope, budget, and schedule.

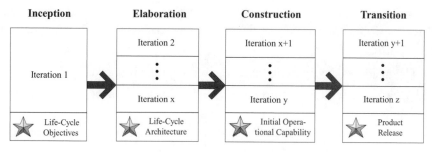

**Figure 1-1: Phases and Major Milestones**

Figure 1-1 shows the phases and major milestones of the Unified Process. In it, you can see that each phase contains one or more iterations. We'll explore the concept of iterations in the section "Iterations and Increments" later in this chapter.

The following subsections describe the key aspects of each of these phases.

## Inception

The primary goal of the **Inception phase** is to establish the case for the viability of the proposed system.

The tasks that a project team performs during Inception include the following:

- Defining the scope of the system (that is, what's in and what's out)
- Outlining a **candidate architecture**, which is made up of initial versions of six different models
- Identifying critical risks and determining when and how the project will address them
- Starting to make the business case that the project is worth doing, based on initial estimates of cost, effort, schedule, and product quality

The concept of candidate architecture is discussed in the section "Architecture-Centric" later in this chapter. The six models are covered in the next major section of this chapter, "The Five Workflows."

The major milestone associated with the Inception phase is called **Life-Cycle Objectives**. The indications that the project has reached this milestone include the following:

- The major stakeholders agree on the scope of the proposed system.
- The candidate architecture clearly addresses a set of critical high-level requirements.
- The business case for the project is strong enough to justify a green light for continued development.

Chapter 7 describes the details of the Inception phase.

## Elaboration

The primary goal of the **Elaboration phase** is to establish the ability to build the new system given the financial constraints, schedule constraints, and other kinds of constraints that the development project faces.

The tasks that a project team performs during Elaboration include the following:

- Capturing a healthy majority of the remaining functional requirements
- Expanding the candidate architecture into a full **architectural baseline**, which is an internal release of the system focused on describing the architecture
- Addressing significant risks on an ongoing basis
- Finalizing the business case for the project and preparing a project plan that contains sufficient detail to guide the next phase of the project (Construction)

The architectural baseline contains expanded versions of the six models initialized during the Inception phase.

The major milestone associated with the Elaboration phase is called **Life-Cycle Architecture**. The indications that the project has reached this milestone include the following:

- Most of the functional requirements for the new system have been captured in the use case model.
- The architectural baseline is a small, skinny system that will serve as a solid foundation for ongoing development.
- The business case has received a green light, and the project team has an initial project plan that describes how the Construction phase will proceed.

The use case model is described in the upcoming section "The Five Work-flows." Risks are discussed in the section "Iterations and Increments" later in this chapter.

Chapter 8 describes the details of the Elaboration phase.

## Construction

The primary goal of the **Construction phase** is to build a system capable of operating successfully in beta customer environments.

During Construction, the project team performs tasks that involve building the system iteratively and incrementally (see "Iterations and Increments" later in this chapter), making sure that the viability of the system is always evident in executable form.

The major milestone associated with the Construction phase is called **Initial Operational Capability**. The project has reached this milestone if a set of beta customers has a more or less fully operational system in their hands.

Chapter 9 describes the details of the Construction phase.

## Transition

The primary goal of the **Transition phase** is to roll out the fully functional system to customers.

During Transition, the project team focuses on correcting defects and modifying the system to correct previously unidentified problems.

The major milestone associated with the Transition phase is called **Product Release**.

Chapter 10 describes the details of the Transition phase.

## The Five Workflows

Within the Unified Process, five **workflows** cut across the set of four phases: Requirements, Analysis, Design, Implementation, and Test. Each workflow is a set of activities that various project workers perform.

The following subsections provide brief overviews of these workflows.

### Requirements

The primary activities of the **Requirements workflow** are aimed at building the use case model, which captures the functional requirements of the system being defined. This model helps the project stakeholders reach agreement on the capabilities of the system and the conditions to which it must conform.

The use case model also serves as the foundation for all other development work. Figure 1-2 shows how the use case model influences the other five models discussed in the subsequent subsections.

Chapter 2 discusses the key aspects of the Requirements workflow. Chapters 7, 8, and 9 describe how this workflow cuts across the Inception, Elaboration, and Construction phases, respectively.

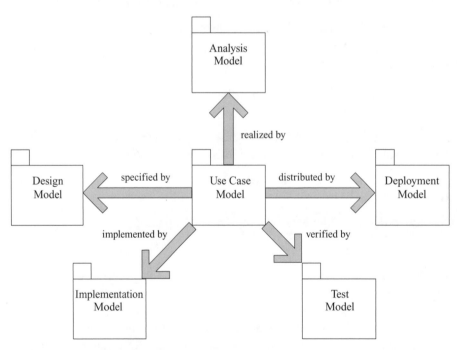

**Figure 1-2: The Six Basic Unified Process Models**

## Analysis

The primary activities of the **Analysis workflow** are aimed at building the analysis model, which helps the developers refine and structure the functional requirements captured within the use case model. This model contains realizations of use cases that lend themselves to design and implementation work better than the use cases.

Chapter 3 discusses the key aspects of the Analysis workflow. Chapters 7, 8, and 9 describe how this workflow cuts across the Inception, Elaboration, and Construction phases, respectively.

## Design

The primary activities of the **Design workflow** are aimed at building the design model, which describes the physical realizations of the use cases from the use case model, and also the contents of the analysis model. The design model serves as an abstraction of the implementation model (see the next subsection).

The Design workflow also focuses on the deployment model, which defines the physical organization of the system in terms of computational nodes.

Chapter 4 discusses the key aspects of the Design workflow. Chapters 7, 8, and 9 describe how this workflow cuts across the Inception, Elaboration, and Construction phases, respectively.

## Implementation

The primary activities of the **Implementation workflow** are aimed at building the implementation model, which describes how the elements of the design model are packaged into software components, such as source code files, dynamic link libraries (DLLs), and EJBs.

Chapter 5 discusses the key aspects of the Implementation workflow. Chapters 8 and 9 describe how this workflow cuts across the Elaboration and Construction phases, respectively.

## Test

The primary activities of the **Test workflow** are aimed at building the test model, which describes how integration and system tests will exercise executable components from the implementation model. The test model also describes how the team will perform those tests as well as unit tests.

The test model contains test cases that are often derived directly from use cases. Testers perform black-box testing using the original use case text, and white-box testing of the realizations of those use cases, as specified within the analysis model. The test model also contains the results of all levels of testing.

Chapter 6 discusses the key aspects of the Test workflow. Chapters 8 and 9 describe how this workflow cuts across the Elaboration and Construction phases, respectively.

## Iterations and Increments

As mentioned in "The Four Phases," each of the Unified Process's phases is divided into iterations. An **iteration** is simply a mini-project that's part of a phase.

A typical iteration crosses all five of the workflows discussed in the previous section, to a greater or lesser extent. For instance, an iteration during the Elaboration phase might focus heavily on activities of the Requirements and Analysis workflows, whereas an iteration during Construction is more likely to involve Design, Implementation, and Test activities. (Chapters 7 through 9 discuss the details of these crossovers.)

Each iteration results in an **increment**. This is a release of the system that contains added or improved functionality compared with the previous release.

Figure 1-3 shows the essence of the iterative and incremental approach to software development.

Using an iterative and incremental approach, a project team starts the development process by evaluating the relevant risks, including those associated with requirements, skills, technology, and politics, and by ensuring that the scope of the project is defined to everyone's satisfaction (see "Elaboration"). Then the team follows these steps:

1. Define the first iteration, addressing the most critical and difficult risks. (In other words, do the hard stuff first.)
2. Map out a plan for the iteration to a suitable level of detail.

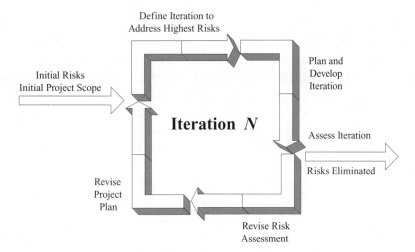

**Figure 1-3: Iterative and Incremental Development**

3.  Perform the appropriate activities; for the Unified Process, these are activities associated with the Requirements, Analysis, Design, Implementation, and Test workflows.

4.  Do a postmortem on the increment that results from the iteration.

5.  Discard the risks that the increment has sufficiently addressed. Then update the ongoing risk list.

6.  Revise the overall project plan in response to the relative success or failure of the iteration.

7.  Proceed with the next iteration.

Iterations build the six models increment by increment. At the end of each iteration, the full set of models that represents the system is in a particular state; this is the architectural baseline.

## Artifacts, Workers, and Activities

The following subsections describe three key elements of each of the workflows within the Unified Process: artifacts, workers, and activities.

## Artifacts

Within the Unified Process, an **artifact** is any meaningful internal or deliverable chunk of information that plays a role in the development of the system. This book focuses on engineering artifacts, which include things like models, the user-interface prototype, and test evaluations. These artifacts are defined within the workflow chapters, and they're also discussed as deliverables of the phases in which they come into play. Management artifacts, such as the business case and the project plan, are also discussed in the contexts of the five workflows and the four phases. One of the underlying premises of the Unified Process is that a system is not considered fully deliverable until the appropriate artifacts, whether for internal use only or for customers, are reasonably complete.

## Workers

The Unified Process defines a **worker** as a role that an individual may play on the project. (The primary difference between a worker and an actor is that an actor is on the outside looking in, whereas a worker is on the inside, perhaps looking out, perhaps not. Also, actors have operational or usage relationships with the system, whereas workers are participants in the development of the system.) Workers produce artifacts, either as individuals or as part of subteams or the team as a whole. One thing to remember is that one person can perform as more than one worker over the course of the project; for example, an analyst may discover use cases and write text for them as well.

## Activities

Each workflow comprises several activities. In the context of a workflow, an **activity** is a task that a worker performs in order to produce an artifact. The activities described in this book range from high-level exploration of the concepts and things of interest to the customers (Build the Domain Model) to highly detailed work related to the physical system (Implement a Class).

# Chapter 2

# The Requirements Workflow

## Introduction

The fundamental principle of the **Requirements workflow** is to work toward *building the right system*. This involves gathering requirements from the various project stakeholders and negotiating those requirements until it's clear that the customers and the development team agree on what features the new system will contain. (Note that the question of *building the system right* is addressed during the other workflows.)

Requirements capture is generally difficult because:

- For all practical purposes, customers and developers speak different languages.
- It's often hard to pin customers down about what they want: they don't know, they think they know but they can't articulate it, they change their minds, they contradict themselves.
- Requirements documents tend to be riddled with ambiguity, redundancy, and internal contradiction.

The Requirements workflow specifies tasks that relate to four key goals of requirements capture. These goals are described in the following subsections.

### Reach Agreement on the System Context

Three useful constructs for helping the stakeholders reach agreement on "what's in and what's out" are domain models, business models, and high-level use case diagrams.

A **domain model** describes the important things and concepts associated with a system in terms of objects. The team can use the domain model to help everyone come to agreement about what needs to be represented within the new system. The subsections "Domain Model" and "Build the Domain Model," which appear later in this chapter, describe the nature of a domain model and how to build one, respectively.

A **business model** describes business processes in terms of customers and conceptual and concrete business objects. This kind of model can be very useful in helping the development team understand the inner workings of the business for which the system will be built. The subsections "Business Model" and "Build the Business Model," which appear later in this chapter, offer detail about business models and how to build them, respectively.

The Unified Process specifies that the use case (see "Identify and Negotiate Functional Requirements," on the next page) is the fundamental unit for capturing functional requirements. **Use case diagrams** show use cases and the people or things that interact with them. Drawing use case diagrams that show broadly defined, high-level use cases (for instance, at what might be called the "executive summary" level, and perhaps a level or two below that) is a relatively quick and easy technique for reaching an understanding of the boundaries of the system being modeled.

### List Candidate Requirements

Every single stakeholder will probably come up with at least a few suggestions about features that the system should offer. A **feature list** is a document that identifies and briefly describes these suggestions, which can be seen as **candidate requirements**. (For planning and management purposes, each feature should also have enough associated information to allow for reasonably good estimates related to schedule and budget.) The team can use the feature list as a frame of reference in deciding which features to map to actual requirements and then address within a given cycle or iteration.

### Identify and Negotiate Functional Requirements

**Use cases** specify sequences of actions that actors (humans or non-human entities that interact with the system from the outside) and the system perform to produce results of value. They offer an excellent way to discover customers' requirements, as well-written use case text closely resembles text that one would find in a good user manual. Use cases, especially when used in conjunction with prototypes of the user interface, also serve as strong support for negotiating requirements with customers, as the development team uses the use case text as leverage to reduce ambiguity and eliminate assumptions, as well as to delineate clearly the boundaries of sets of use cases that will be built during a given iteration of the system. Later in this chapter, the subsection "Use Case" discusses use cases in more detail; "Find Actors and Use Cases" and "Detail a Use Case" describe how to discover actors and use cases and write good use case text, respectively.

### Specify Nonfunctional Requirements

Nonfunctional requirements are associated with issues such as performance, security, scalability, and reliability. These are the key drivers of the architecture, along with certain of the use cases. While performing the various Requirements workflow activities, the development team can capture these requirements within the domain model by, for example, assigning permitted values to attributes on classes. Using UML constructs such as the **constraint** (a condition that must hold true) and the use case model as supplementary information connected with individual use cases or groups of use cases also helps capture these requirements. The section "Supplementary Requirements," which appears later in this chapter, describes requirements that don't easily trace to specific use cases.

## Artifacts

The following subsections describe the various artifacts that may be generated within the Requirements workflow.

## Domain Model

The **domain model** captures the important real-world things and concepts that belong to the problem space, which defines the problem that the new system is being built to solve. These things and concepts are represented as **classes** and the various kinds of relationships among them.

The UML **class diagram** is the most common vehicle for capturing the contents of the domain model. Figure 2-1 shows a class diagram that includes a number of classes and relationships of relevance to The Internet Bookstore.

 See Chapter 3 of *UML Explained* for more information about the elements of this class diagram.

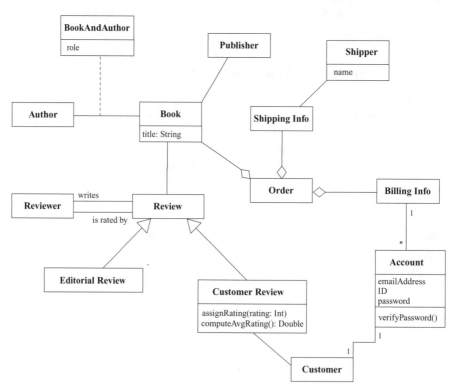

**Figure 2-1: Class Diagram**

Note that this diagram doesn't contain too many details. A term that's sometimes used for this kind of diagram is **domain-level class diagram**. Upcoming chapters contain domain-level class diagrams that show more detail.

## Business Model

Within the Unified Process, the term **business model** refers to a pair of models: the business object model and the business use case model.

A **business use case model** contains **business use cases**, which describe business processes, and **business actors**, which describe customers and partners. There are direct correlations between business use cases and "regular" use cases (see "Use Case" later in this chapter), and between business actors and regular actors (see "Actor" later in this chapter); in fact, both kinds of use cases and actors appear on UML use case diagrams, an example of which appears in the section "Find Actors and Use Cases" later in this chapter.

A **business object model** describes how the business use cases are "realized" by a set of workers using **business entities** (which can be conceptual things, such as accounts, or concrete things, like forms). This model also describes **work units**, which are sets of business entities. Business entities and work units often represent the same kinds of concepts and things that classes do in the domain model, so the business object model is generally expressed in domain-level class diagrams and other, more detailed types of diagrams that are discussed in upcoming chapters.

See *The Object Advantage: Business Process Reengineering with Object Technology* (Ivar Jacobson, Maria Ericsson, and Agneta Jacobson; Addison-Wesley, 1995) for an extensive discussion of business modeling.

## Glossary

The **glossary** contains the various key terms, specific to the system, used in the other project artifacts. These terms can describe concrete things as well as abstract things and concepts. The objective is for project stakeholders to use the glossary to help reach common agreement about what things are called. The glossary is often derived from the domain model, the business model, or both.

## Actor

An **actor** represents one of two things:

- A role that a user can play with regard to the system
- An entity, such as another system or a database, that resides outside the system

Note that the name of an actor should *not* be that of a particular person; instead, it should identify a role or set of roles that a human being, an external system, or a part of the system being built will play relative to one or more use cases. If you have a business model, actors generally correspond with the workers in that model.

You show an actor as a stick figure with a short descriptive name. Figure 2-2 shows some of the human and non-human actors that might interact with The Internet Bookstore.

## Use Case

A **use case** is a sequence of actions that an actor performs in conjunction with a system to achieve a particular goal.

A use case should describe one aspect of usage of the system without presuming any specific design or implementation. In other words, a use case describes *what* the system needs to do without specifying *how* the system will perform.

You show a use case as an ellipse with a short name that contains an active verb and (usually) a noun phrase. The name of a use case can appear either within the ellipse or below it. Figure 2-3 shows some of the use cases for our bookstore.

Customer        Shipping System        Accountant

**Figure 2-2: Actors**

**Figure 2-3: Use Cases**

The text of a use case describes possible paths through the use case. This text includes the actions that the actor performs and the system's responses to those actions. You capture these paths as **flows of events**.

Two kinds of flows of events are associated with use cases.

- The **main flow of events** (sometimes referred to as the **basic course of action**) is the sunny-day scenario, the main start-to-finish path that the actor and the system will follow under normal circumstances. The assumption is that the actor doesn't make any mistakes, and the system generates no errors. A use case always has a main flow of events.

- An **exceptional flow of events** (or **alternate course of action**) is a path through a use case that represents an error condition or a path that the actor and the system take less frequently. A use case often has at least one exceptional flow of events; in fact, the more interesting behavior described by use cases is often found in the alternate courses.

## User-Interface Prototype

User-interface (UI) prototypes help the developers shape the look and feel of the system with the customers and also help the developers understand certain of the customers' requirements. Within the Unified Process, a UI prototype can take any form ranging from sketches on a piece of paper to a set of storyboards to fully operational interactive prototypes. Regardless of which form these prototypes take, though, they are likely to serve as an excellent source of material for use cases.

## Use Case Model

A UML **package** is a grouping of pieces of a model. A package can itself contain packages. The **use case model** is basically a package of use case packages, each of which contain actors and use cases.

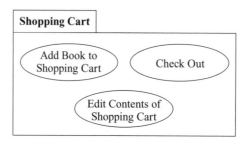

**Figure 2-4: Use Case Package**

In a diagram, a UML package appears as a tabbed folder. There are two variations:

- The name of the package appears within the tab, and the contents of the package are listed in the body of the folder.
- The package name appears in the body of the folder, and the contents are hidden from view.

Figure 2-4 shows the initial contents of a use case package for our on-line bookstore.

 See "Packages and Use Cases" in Chapter 4 of *UML Explained* for more information about this use case package.

## Architecture Description (View of the Use Case Model)

Part of the architecture description is a view of the use case model that contains the architecturally significant use cases. These are the use cases that describe important functionality, address particularly significant requirements, or both.

## Supplementary Requirements

A **supplementary requirement** is a nonfunctional requirement. This kind of requirement deals with issues such as performance, security, and backup, or constraints imposed from outside the system, such as those involving regulatory agencies. A supplementary requirement tends not to match up with a particular use case; it may be addressed by several use cases, though.

## Workers

The following subsections describe the various workers that play key roles within the Requirements workflow. (Remember that a worker is a logical role, not a physical person, in this context.)

### System Analyst

A **system analyst** focuses on capturing the requirements related to the use cases. This involves the following:

- Leading the effort to build the domain model and the business model (see "Build the Domain Model" and "Build the Business Model" later in this chapter)
- Finding the actors and the use cases (see "Find Actors and Use Cases" later in this chapter)
- Ensuring the completeness and consistency of the use case model as a whole (see "Structure the Use Case Model" later in this chapter)

A system analyst is also likely to have primary responsibility for the glossary (see "Glossary" earlier in this chapter).

### Use Case Specifier

A **use case specifier** writes the detailed descriptions of the main and exceptional flows of events for one or more use cases (see "Detail a Use Case" later in this chapter).

### User-Interface Designer

A **user-interface designer** provides the visual shaping of those elements of the user interface that one or more actors will use. This usually involves designing the user-interface prototype to start (see "Prototype the User Interface" later in this chapter).

## Architect

Within the Requirements workflow, an **architect** prioritizes the given set of use cases (see "Prioritize the Use Cases" later in this chapter) and includes the architecturally significant use cases in the architecture description (see "Architecture Description (View of the Use Case Model)" earlier in this chapter).

## Activities

Figure 2-5 shows the various activities that workers perform within the Requirements workflow.

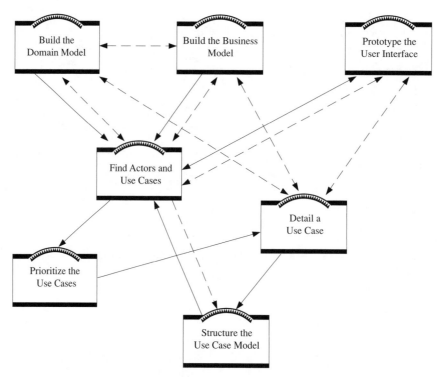

**Figure 2-5: Requirements Workflow Activities**

The following subsections describe these activities.

### Build the Domain Model

This activity involves understanding and describing the most important classes that represent the problem space, and also the relationships among those classes, at a fairly high level of abstraction. A system analyst (see "System Analyst" earlier in this chapter) generally has the responsibility of leading work on this activity.

Initial domain modeling can occur effectively in various contexts. When domain experts are available, brainstorming sessions, within which one person serves as the moderator/facilitator and another captures the results of the discussions on class diagrams, can be highly productive. Another approach involves mining available documentation, such as the problem statement and low-level requirements (and legacy documentation, for a reengineering project), for candidate classes, using a technique called **grammatical inspection** or **noun-verb analysis**. This involves circling or highlighting nouns that might become classes and verbs that might become associations between classes. (This technique is demonstrated in *Use Case Driven Object Modeling with UML*. See Appendix C for more information on the process this book describes.)

Domain modeling continues as the analysts decide which candidate classes should become actual classes and which candidate associations should become actual associations. Domain modelers also make initial decisions about generalization and aggregation relationships among classes at this point. These are *only* initial decisions: The contents of the domain model will undergo considerable refinement and expansion as development work proceeds, so it's important to remember that the class diagrams that make up the domain model need to stay in synch with the customers' understanding of the problem space. These diagrams shouldn't get bogged down with details that customers don't need to see.

The project team should aspire to these three goals:

- Help everyone on the project team reach agreement on the names of things and concepts of relevance to the system being developed.

- Produce a glossary (see "Glossary" earlier in this chapter) of class names that can serve as nouns within use case text.

- Build a set of class diagrams that work together to serve as a solid foundation for the Analysis workflow (the subject of the next chapter).

Figure 2-5 shows the following:

- The Build the Domain Model activity can occur in parallel with the Build the Business Model activity (see below), with the domain model and the business model influencing each other.
- The domain model provides a good starting point for finding actors and use cases; as those elements are explored, the domain model tends to be expanded and refined in response.
- The team can also improve the domain model as they're writing use case text, with the goal of having the model and the text closely in synch.

### Build the Business Model

This activity involves building a business use case model and a business object model, so the project team can understand the workings of the business they're modeling in terms of both internal workflows and external stimuli that influence the business's behaviors. A system analyst (see "System Analyst" earlier in this chapter) generally has the responsibility of leading work on this activity.

You can think of a business object model as an expanded version of the domain model. A good business use case model is the source of a healthy number of actors and use cases, which helps fuel the next activity in this workflow.

As you can see from Figure 2-5, the business model has the same kinds of relationships with other activities in this workflow as the domain model.

### Find Actors and Use Cases

This activity involves discovering the human and non-human actors that will be interacting with the system, and putting together a set of use cases that reflect the behavior that those actors will be performing in conjunction with the system. A system analyst (see "System Analyst" earlier in this chapter) is responsible for performing this activity.

Business models (see the previous section) and prototypes (see the next section) are generally excellent sources of actors and use cases. Other good places to find actors include the domain model, high-level requirements, and context diagrams that show the external systems with which the new system will work. In many cases, exploration and negotiation of use cases occurs in workshops that involve representatives of the customers and the development team; doing these workshops using guidelines such as those offered by joint application development (JAD) should yield positive results.

The UML **use case diagram** shows actors, use cases, and the relationships among them. Figure 2-6 shows a use case diagram for The Internet Bookstore.

 See "Use Case Diagrams" in Chapter 4 of *UML Explained* for more about use case diagrams.

It's useful to try to capture the essence of each actor and each use case in the form of a brief description. The team shouldn't start writing the detailed use case text at this point, though; that's the focus of the Detail a Use Case activity, which is described later in this chapter.

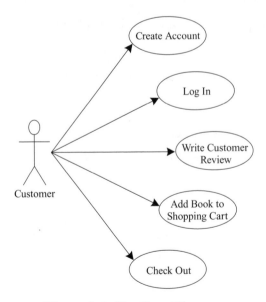

**Figure 2-6: Use Case Diagram**

As actors and use cases get added to the use case model, it's necessary to ensure that the model remains internally consistent and easy to understand. Breaking the model into packages (see "Use Case Model" earlier in this chapter) will help the team achieve these objectives; well-defined use case packages can also be very useful in dividing up use case modeling tasks among sets of workers.

The total set of actors within a complete use case model, which comes together after all iterations of this activity, should reflect everything that needs to exchange information with the system being modeled. The total set of use cases within that model should capture all of the functional requirements that the system's stakeholders have put forth.

In the course of capturing functional requirements in the form of use cases, supplementary requirements will also crop up. There are various ways to capture these nonfunctional requirements outside the use case model. In doing so, it's important to remember is that there needs to be traceability between these requirements and the other models, especially the implementation model (discussed in Chapter 5). See *Managing Software Requirements: A Unified Approach* (Leffingwell and Widrig; Addison-Wesley, 2000) for an expansive discussion of an approach to managing requirements that dovetails nicely with the Unified Process.

A second, related term, **special requirement**, refers to a nonfunctional requirement that the team needs to address at some point during a workflow subsequent to the one in which they're currently operating. Special requirements are discussed further in the chapters that describe the phases of the Unified Process.

### Prototype the User Interface

A user-interface designer (see "User-Interface Designer" earlier in this chapter) is responsible for building the UI prototypes.

Prototypes at any level of sophistication will generally offer the team significant help in finding actors and use cases and in writing the text for use cases. (The use cases are likely to influence the development of the prototypes as well, as indicated in Figure 2-5.) They also serve as an excellent source of classes and attributes belonging to those classes, as areas of GUI windows or screens tend to match up more or less directly with elements of the domain model.

## Prioritize the Use Cases

This activity involves assigning priorities, based on both technical and non-technical considerations, to the various use cases. An architect (see "Architect" earlier in this chapter) is responsible for performing this activity.

The resulting list will help dictate which use cases the development team should focus on during early iterations, and which ones can be postponed. The use cases with the highest priorities generally become part of the architecture description (see the section "Architecture Description (View of the Use Case Model)" earlier in this chapter).

## Detail a Use Case

This activity involves writing text for the basic course of action and alternate courses of action (see "Use Case" earlier in this chapter) for a use case. A use case specifier (see "Use Case Specifier" earlier in this chapter) performs this activity.

The text for the basic course of action for a good use case should typically be between one and three paragraphs long; the text for alternate courses should be a sentence or two for each course on average. The idea is for each use case to address one or more requirements in text that's easy to understand quickly for everyone involved in the project, whether technically savvy or not. (It may be the case that more than one use case is necessary to capture a requirement.)

Here are some more qualities of an effective use case:

*   It's written in active voice and present tense.
*   It names the elements of the interface (see "User-Interface Prototype" earlier in this chapter) that the main actor uses in interacting with the system, as well as the relevant classes from the domain model (see "Domain Model" earlier in this chapter).
*   It's easy to see how the alternate courses tie in with the basic course.

The following text describes the basic course of action and alternate courses of action of the Log In use case within the use case model for The Internet Bookstore.

> **Main flow of events**: The Customer clicks the Login button on the Home Page. The system displays the Login Page. The Customer enters his or her user ID and password, and then clicks the OK button. The system validates the login information against the persistent Account data, and then returns the Customer to the Home Page.

> **Exceptional flow of events**: If the Customer clicks the New Account button, the system displays the Create New Account page.

> **Exceptional flow of events**: If the Customer clicks the Reminder Word button, the system displays the reminder word stored for that Customer, in a separate dialog box. When the Customer clicks the OK button, the system returns the Customer to the Home Page.

> **Exceptional flow of events**: If the Customer enters a user ID that the system does not recognize, the system displays the Create New Account page.

> **Exceptional flow of events**: If the Customer enters an incorrect password, the system prompts the Customer to reenter his or her password.

> **Exceptional flow of events**: If the Customer enters an incorrect password three times, the system displays a page telling the Customer that he or she should contact customer service.

 See Chapter 4 of *UML Explained* for more information about this use case.

The UML activity diagram, an example of which appears in Chapter 4 (see the section "Design Class"), can also be very helpful in describing a use case, especially when the text contains a relatively large number of possible paths. The basic rule here is that if you think a flowchart might add value to your use case over and above the text, draw an activity diagram.

## Structure the Use Case Model

This activity involves breaking up use cases in search of simpler ones. A system analyst (see "System Analyst" earlier in this chapter) is responsible for performing this activity.

The UML offers three constructs for factoring out common behavior and variant paths.

- Within an **include** relationship, one use case *explicitly* includes the behavior of another use case at a specified point within a course of action. The included use case doesn't stand alone; it has to be connected with one or more base use cases. The include mechanism is very useful for factoring out behavior that would otherwise appear within multiple use cases.

  Within Figure 2-7, the Add to Wish List and Check Out use cases include the behavior captured within the Log In use case because a Customer of The Internet Bookstore must be logged in before he or she can add a book to a wish list or make a purchase.

- Within an **extend** relationship, a base use case *implicitly* includes the behavior of another use case at one or more specified points. These points are called **extension points**. You generally use this construct to factor out behavior that's optional or that occurs only under certain conditions. One way to use "extends" is in creating a new use case in response to an alternate course of action having several steps associated with it.

  Figure 2-8 shows that a Customer of our bookstore has the option of canceling an Order in conjunction with checking the status of that Order.

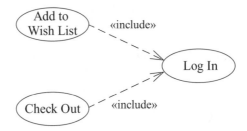

**Figure 2-7: Include Relationships**

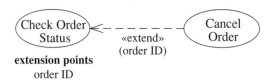

**Figure 2-8: Extend Relationship**

- Generalization works the same way for use cases as it does for classes: A parent use case defines behavior that its children can inherit, and the children can add to or override that behavior.

Figure 2-9 shows use cases that describe three different searches that a bookstore Customer can perform, all of which use the basic search technique defined by the Perform Search use case.

The team should also feel free to use other techniques. For instance, the Open Modeling Language (OML) defines two constructs, **invokes** and **precedes**, that may work better for some people than the UML constructs for structuring the use case model. See *Use Case Driven Object Modeling with UML* for more information about these constructs.

**Figure 2-9: Use Case Generalization**

# Chapter 3

# The Analysis Workflow

## Introduction

In the **Analysis workflow**, the development team's fundamental goal is to gain real understanding of the customers' requirements and to use that understanding to build momentum as the project heads into design and implementation. The primary result of this workflow is the **analysis model**, which is meant to help the team start pursuing other goals, such as resource sharing, maintainability, resiliency, and reuse.

The analysis model represents a refinement and expansion of the use case model (see "Use Case Model" in Chapter 2). The nature of this refinement and expansion can be summarized as follows:

- Even the most rigorous use case modeling effort is likely to have loose ends, in the form of text that's not quite precise enough, or forgotten alternate courses of action. Performing a proper analysis of the use case model should result in the virtual elimination of these kinds of flaws in that model.

- Analysis enables the development team to start addressing issues such as the distribution of objects, concurrency, and performance, which are generally not dealt with during initial use case modeling efforts.

- Within the Unified Process, analysis represents the part of a project where the focus starts shifting away from customers and toward what the developers need to do in order to *build the system right*. Whereas customers should be consulted (or at least represented) during all facets of the Requirements workflow, customer involvement in the Analysis workflow is necessary only in cases where significant negotiation about requirements still needs to occur.

## Artifacts

The following subsections describe the various artifacts that may be generated within the Analysis workflow.

### Analysis Class

An **analysis class** is a class specified to the level of detail appropriate to the Analysis workflow, which generally means that it contains attributes but not operations. These attributes usually reflect characteristics of things and concepts represented in the domain model (see "Domain Model" in Chapter 2) and the business model (see "Business Model," also in Chapter 2). Note, though, that even though an analysis class exists at a lower level of abstraction than a class from the domain model, it's still more conceptual than physical.

There are three types of analysis classes: **boundary classes**, **entity classes**, and **control classes**. The following text describes these types of classes in terms of instances of the classes (in other words, **objects**).

- A **boundary object** is an object with which an actor interacts. If the actor is human, the boundary object is likely to be a window, HTML page, dialog box, or menu. A non-human actor interacts with boundary objects such as application program interfaces (APIs). Boundary objects correspond with nouns in use case text (see "Use Case" in Chapter 2).

Figure 3-1 shows the symbol for a boundary object.

**Figure 3-1: Boundary Object**

- An **entity object** is generally an object that contains long-lived information, such as that associated with databases. In many cases, entity objects come directly from the domain model or the business model. An entity object can also contain transient data, such as the contents of lists in windows or search results. Entity objects correspond with nouns in use case text.

  Figure 3-2 shows the symbol for an entity object.

**Figure 3-2: Entity Object**

- A **control object** is an object that embodies application logic. Control objects are often used to handle things such as coordination and sequencing. They are also useful for calculations involving multiple entity objects.

  Control objects serve as the connecting tissue between boundary objects and entity objects. They correspond with verbs in use case text.

  Figure 3-3 shows the symbol for a control object.

**Figure 3-3: Control Object**

The next section contains examples of all three types of analysis objects.

## Use Case Realization–Analysis

A **use case realization–analysis** is a collaboration that describes how the actor(s) and the system perform a given use case, in terms of analysis classes. (A **collaboration** is a collection of classes and other elements that work together to provide some behavior.) A development team produces use case realizations–analysis by performing **robustness analysis**, which involves looking at each sentence of a use case; determining the boundary, entity, and control objects that it needs in order to address the behavior it specifies; and drawing those objects and their relationships.

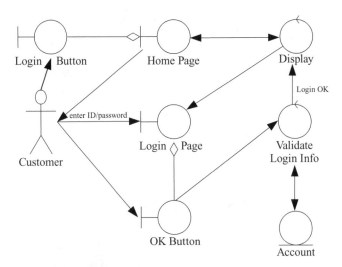

**Figure 3-4: Robustness Diagram**

A **robustness diagram** is a special form of UML collaboration diagram that contains a use case realization–analysis. Figure 3-4 shows a robustness diagram for the analysis-level realization of the main flow of events for a use case called Log In.

 See "Putting Analysis Objects Together" in Chapter 5 of *UML Explained* for more about this robustness diagram.

Analysis classes that match up with classes in the domain model appear on what we might call analysis-level class diagrams. (See Figure 2-1 in Chapter 2 for an example of a class diagram.) Other analysis classes that don't already appear on class diagrams connected with the domain model, such as (a) classes to which "transient" entity objects (objects that are only "alive" for, say, the time it takes to execute a use case) and (b) classes to which boundary objects belong, will generally appear on separate class diagrams. (Note that an analysis class can participate in one or more use case realizations–analysis.) An example of an analysis-level class diagram appears in Chapter 8.

**Figure 3-5: Use Case Realization–Analysis**

The symbol for a collaboration is the same as that of a use case, except that the border of the oval is dashed instead of solid. Figure 3-5 shows how we would show the use case realization—analysis associated with the Log In use case using UML notation.

 See "Collaborations" in Chapter 9 of *UML Explained* for more about collaborations.

See *Use Case Driven Object Modeling with UML* for a more extensive discussion of robustness analysis.

## Analysis Package

An **analysis package** is a UML package that contains analysis classes and use case realizations–analysis. An analysis package can also contain other analysis packages.

The Unified Process also defines a special type of analysis package, called a **service package**, that models a **service**, which is an atomic (indivisible) chunk of functionality that appears in one or more use cases. The team uses service packages to define sets of features that it can treat as discrete units as development proceeds through design and implementation. Service packages are also useful in helping the development team focus on opportunities to reuse analysis classes across realizations and, perhaps, within other systems.

Figure 3-6 shows some of the contents of an analysis package that contains elements related to customers of our on-line bookstore.

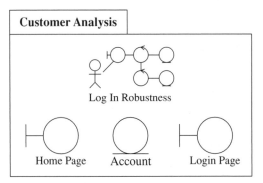

**Figure 3-6: Analysis Package**

 See "Analysis Packages and Design Packages" in Chapter 5 of *UML Explained* for more about this analysis package.

## Analysis Model

The **analysis model** is basically a package of analysis packages. This model can be considered correct when it contains all of the use case realizations–analysis and associated analysis classes required to realize the functionality specified by the use cases contained within the use case model (see "User-Interface Prototype" in Chapter 2).

## Architecture Description (View of the Analysis Model)

Part of the architecture description is a view of the analysis model that contains the architecturally significant elements of that model. This generally includes the following:

- The analysis packages and the relationships among them
- The use case realizations–analysis that correspond with the architecturally significant use cases from the use case model
- The analysis classes that participate in those realizations

# Workers

The following subsections describe the various workers that play key roles within the Analysis workflow. (Remember that in this context, a worker is a logical role, not a physical person.)

## Architect

Within the Analysis workflow, the architect is responsible for the following:

- Outlining the analysis model in terms of initial analysis packages and analysis classes (see "Perform Architectural Analysis" later in this chapter)
- Ensuring the completeness and correctness of the analysis model as a whole
- Identifying the architecturally significant use case realizations–analysis and analysis classes and including them in the architecture description (see "Architecture Description (View of the Analysis Model)" earlier in this chapter).

 See "Architect" in Chapter 2 for information about other roles that the architect plays within the Unified Process.

## Use Case Engineer

Within the Analysis workflow, a use case engineer builds one or more use case realizations–analysis (see "Analyze a Use Case" later in this chapter). This includes defining outline versions of the analysis classes that come into play during these realizations.

## Component Engineer

Within the Analysis workflow, a component engineer is responsible for the full definitions of one or more analysis classes and for the contents of one or more analysis packages (see "Analyze a Class" and "Analyze a Package" later in this chapter). This includes ensuring that the analysis classes and use case realizations–analysis defined by the use case engineer(s) work well together.

## Activities

Figure 3-7 shows the various activities that workers perform within the Analysis workflow.

The following subsections describe these activities.

### Perform Architectural Analysis

This activity involves creating outlines of the analysis model and of the architecture as a whole. An architect (see "Architect" earlier in this chapter) is responsible for performing this activity.

As was discussed in the section "Analysis Model" earlier in this chapter, the analysis model is comprised of analysis packages. Architectural analysis involves identifying a first cut of packages that will contain the use case realizations–analysis and analysis classes that the development team will define while performing the activities Analyze a Use Case and Analyze a Class (both of which are described in upcoming sections).

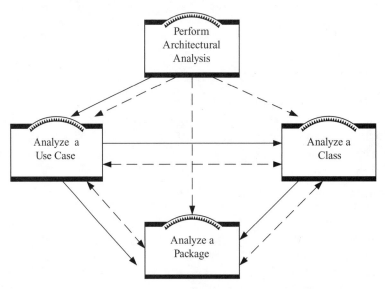

**Figure 3-7: Analysis Workflow Activities**

Analysis packages can evolve in a straightforward manner from well-defined use case packages that make up the use case model (see "Use Case Model" in Chapter 2). Similarly, service packages tend to map to services that the architect can form from chunks of functionality that cut across use cases. Two qualities of a good set of analysis packages are high cohesion (each package contains tightly related elements) and loose coupling (there are minimal dependencies among packages).

The architect is also responsible for identifying special requirements that cut across use case realizations–analysis and analysis classes.

### Analyze a Use Case

This activity involves building a use case realization–analysis for a use case. The resulting robustness diagram (see Figure 3-4 earlier in this chapter for an example) identifies objects that belong to analysis classes and the relationships among those classes. A use case engineer (see "Use Case Engineer" earlier in this chapter) is responsible for performing this activity.

An interesting thing about a robustness diagram is that it's often hard to see the flow of control just by looking at the diagram, but it's easy, on a good robustness diagram, to trace the flow of the associated use case. In fact, tracing your finger through the diagram while you read the text of the use case is an excellent way to check the quality of the diagram *and* of the use case. It's likely that the team will want to revisit activities such as Detail a Use Case and Structure the Use Case Model (see Chapter 2) in order to make improvements to the given use case and to the use case model as a whole in response to this quality check.

The use case engineer is also responsible for identifying special requirements relevant to the given realization.

The architect captures the architecturally interesting use case realizations–analysis in the architecture description (see "Architecture Description (View of the Analysis Model)" earlier in this chapter).

### Analyze a Class

This activity involves expanding the definition of an analysis class that participates in one or more use case realizations–analysis. A component engineer (see "Component Engineer" earlier in this chapter) is responsible for performing this activity.

The best approach to defining an analysis class, especially an entity class, involves identifying the responsibilities that the class has across a set of use case realizations, and making decisions based on which class has which responsibilities. This will help the development team build classes that are highly cohesive (operations and attributes work well together, and the class is conceptually "tight") and loosely coupled (classes have minimal dependencies on each other).

It's too early to start assigning operations, but it's a good idea to strive for a rich set of attributes for each analysis class as part of this activity. The user interface will generally serve as a good source: fields on HTML pages, for example, tend to match up well with attributes. This is also where the team refines and expands upon the various kinds of relationships that each analysis class is involved in, with particular focus on aggregations and generalizations. In addition, the definition of an analysis class should address any special requirements associated with the given class.

The architect captures the architecturally interesting analysis classes in the architecture description (see "Architecture Description (View of the Analysis Model)" earlier in this chapter).

## Analyze a Package

This activity involves building an analysis package that was defined during architectural analysis. The goal is a highly cohesive package (in other words, one that contains a set of analysis classes and use case realizations–analysis that are functionally related to a meaningful extent) that is loosely coupled with other packages (that is, dependencies of this package on other packages are minimized). A component engineer (see "Component Engineer" earlier in this chapter) is responsible for performing this activity.

Well-defined analysis packages can be very useful in dividing up analysis tasks among sets of workers, especially if the traceability between these packages and associated use case packages (see "User-Interface Prototype" in Chapter 2) is fairly high.

The architect captures the changes to the analysis packages in the architecture description (see "Architecture Description (View of the Analysis Model)" earlier in this chapter) and ensures that the changes don't threaten the integrity of the architecture.

# Chapter 4

# The Design Workflow

## Introduction

The fundamental goal of the **Design workflow** is for the development team to build a blueprint of the system that the team can rely on going forward into implementation. The primary results of this workflow are the **design model** and the **deployment model**. The design model contains the initial decisions the team makes about issues such as distribution of objects, concurrency, databases, the user interface, transactions, and so forth. The deployment model specifies the geographical distribution of the various pieces of hardware on which the system will be built.

The design model and the deployment model, taken together, represent a refinement and expansion of the analysis model (see "Analysis Model" in Chapter 3). The nature of this refinement and expansion can be summarized as follows:

- The analysis model is still mostly conceptual; the team performing the analysis is likely to have started considering implementation issues, but not to any meaningful extent. The design model is mostly physical: it translates the concepts presented within the analysis model into model elements that closely reflect how the system will be implemented (for instance, by specifying the signatures of operations in the programming language to be used).

- The design model tends to contain considerably more detail than the analysis model, particularly in terms of specifics about how the various objects work together to perform the desired behavior specified by the use case model.

- Whereas the analysis model reflects the team's initial thoughts about what kinds of objects will go on what tiers or layers, the deployment model shows the decisions that the team has made along those lines.

## Artifacts

The following subsections describe the various artifacts that may be generated within the Design workflow.

### Design Class

A **design class** is a class specified to the level of detail appropriate to the Design workflow, which generally means that a design class contains a full set of attributes and operations and a richer set of details about things like visibility.

Where an analysis class (see "Analysis Class" in Chapter 3) is still fairly conceptual, a design class is more physical. In fact, the various parts of design classes are generally expressed in the programming language in which the classes will be implemented. Modelers also address the subject of concurrency by specifying which design classes are **active classes**, instances of which can own processes or threads.

 See "Processes, Threads, and Active Objects" in Chapter 7 of *UML Explained* for more about active classes.

Two UML diagrams can be very useful during the exploration of the nature of a design class: the activity diagram and the statechart (or state) diagram.

An **activity diagram** shows the flows among the various activities that an object performs. This includes the transitions between activities, as well as the branching and merging of paths, that a traditional flowchart shows. It also includes forks and joins, which represent the splitting and synchronization, respectively, of flows of control, each of which operates independent of, and concurrent with, the others. Forks and joins are particularly useful in modeling processes and threads. Figure 4-1 shows part of an activity diagram relevant to our bookstore example.

See "Activity Diagrams" in Chapter 7 of *UML Explained* for more about activity diagrams.

A UML **statechart diagram** (also known as a **state diagram**) shows the different states that an object can assume during its life, the transitions that can happen between those states, and the various kinds of events that the object can respond to, as well as the nature of those responses. State diagrams are especially useful in connection with control objects (see "Analysis Class" in Chapter 3) that embody complicated behavior related to things like traffic control or scheduling. Figure 4-2 shows part of a statechart diagram for our on-line bookstore's Order object.

See "State Machines and Statechart Diagrams" in Chapter 8 of *UML Explained* for more about statechart diagrams.

A **use case realization–design** is a collaboration that describes how the actor(s) and the system perform a given use case, in terms of design classes. A given use case realization–design represents the physical realization of a particular use case realization–analysis and, by extension, of the associated use case.

Two UML diagrams are particularly useful in expressing use case realizations–design: the sequence diagram and the collaboration diagram.

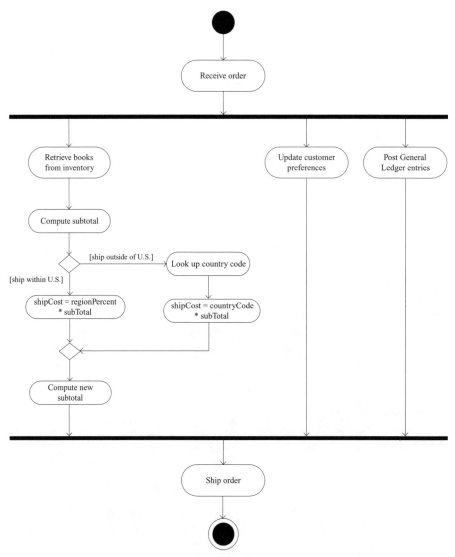

**Figure 4-1: Activity Diagram**

## Use Case Realization–Design

The UML **sequence diagram** focuses on the time ordering of the messages that go back and forth between objects. A development team can use sequence

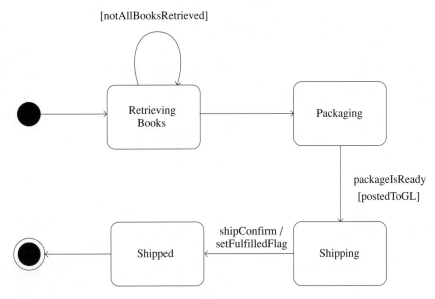

**Figure 4-2: Statechart (State) Diagram**

diagrams in deciding where to assign operations on classes, based on the methods that they assign to objects on the diagram. Figure 4-3 shows the full sequence diagram for the basic course of a use case, called Log In, of relevance to our bookstore.

 See "Sequence Diagrams" in Chapter 5 of *UML Explained* for more about sequence diagrams.

The UML **collaboration diagram** focuses on the organization of the objects that participate in a given set of messages. Collaboration diagrams and sequence diagrams show the same information, but collaboration diagrams can include sequence numbers, which indicate the order in which messages are sent, and they're also better at showing iteration. Figure 4-4 shows what the collaboration diagram might look like for the Log In use case.

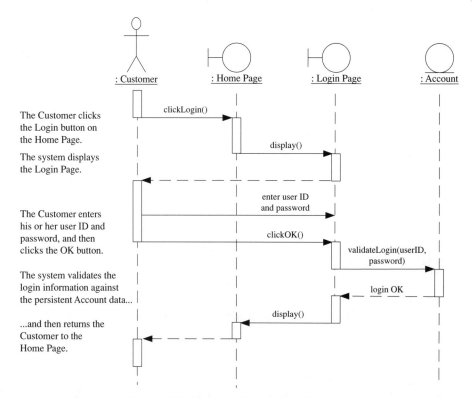

**Figure 4-3: Log In Sequence Diagram**

 See "Collaboration Diagrams" in Chapter 5 of *UML Explained* for more about collaboration diagrams.

Design classes appear on what we might call **design-level class diagrams**. (Note that a design class can participate in one or more use case realizations–design.) An example of a design-level class diagram appears in Chapter 8.

The notation for a use case realization–design is the same for that of a use case realization–analysis (see Figure 3-5 in Chapter 3).

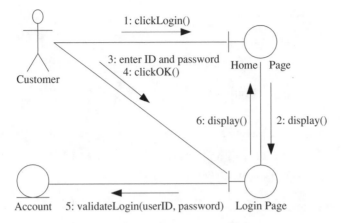

**Figure 4-4: Collaboration Diagram**

## Interface

An **interface** is a collection of operations that represent services offered by a class, subsystem, or component. (Subsystems are discussed in the next section. A discussion of components appears in the next chapter.)

One of the key tenets of object orientation is the separation of an interface from the details of how the exposed operations are implemented. The interface specifies something like a contract that a class must adhere to; the class **realizes** (or provides a **realization** for) one or more interfaces.

The UML provides two ways to show an interface. One way is called lollipop notation; the interface is a circle attached to a class with a straight line. The other way involves defining the interface using a class box and the «interface» stereotype, which is built into the UML, and drawing a dashed line with an open triangle at the end with the interface. Figure 4-5 shows two interfaces of interest to our on-line bookstore.

**Figure 4-5: Class Interfaces**

 See "Interfaces and Classes" in Chapter 6 of *UML Explained* for more about class interfaces.

## Design Subsystem

A **design subsystem** is a UML package that contains design classes, class and subsystem interfaces, and use case realizations–design. A design subsystem can also contain other design subsystems. A given design subsystem should trace directly to one or more analysis packages (see "Analysis Package" in Chapter 3). Design subsystems can also be helpful in incorporating elements of legacy systems into the system being designed, via the well-established technique referred to as wrapping.

The Unified Process also defines a special type of design subsystem, called a **service subsystem**, that models a service at the design level in a way comparable to the way a service package models that service at the analysis level. The product team uses service subsystems to define sets of features that it can treat as discrete units as development proceeds through implementation. Service subsystems are also useful in helping the development team focus on opportunities to reuse design classes in other contexts and across systems.

## Design Model

The **design model** is basically a package of what might be called design packages. This model can be considered correct when it contains all of the use case realizations–design, and associated design classes, required to realize the functionality specified by the use cases contained within the use case model (see "User-Interface Prototype" in Chapter 2), the contents of the analysis model (see "Analysis Model" in Chapter 3), and the supplementary requirements (see "Supplementary Requirements" in Chapter 2).

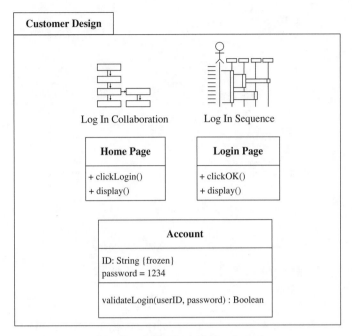

**Figure 4-6: Design Package**

Figure 4-6 and Figure 4-7 show design packages that might belong to the design model for our bookstore.

## Architecture Description (View of the Design Model)

Part of the architecture description is a view of the design model that contains the architecturally significant elements of that model. This generally includes the following:

- The design subsystems, including their interfaces, and the relationships among the subsystems
- The use case realizations–design that correspond with the architecturally significant use cases from the use case model (see "User-Interface Prototype" in Chapter 2) and the associated use case realizations–analysis from the analysis model (see "Analysis Model" in Chapter 3)
- The design classes that participate in those realizations

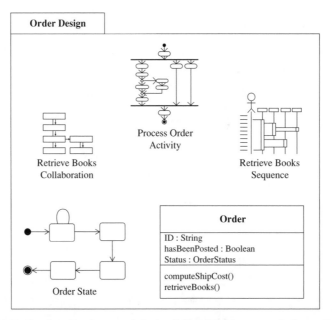

**Figure 4-7: Design Package with Activity Diagram and State Diagram**

## Deployment Model

The **deployment model** defines the physical organization of the system in terms of computational nodes. A **node** is a piece of hardware that represents some kind of computational resource. A physical node generally has memory; it may have processing capability.

Nodes represent the physical deployment of components across the system's hardware. Another way to look at this is that components "live" on nodes. (See "Component" in Chapter 5 for descriptions of the various types of components that the UML supports.)

The UML notation for a node is a cube. Figure 4-8 shows two nodes that form part of our bookstore system.

The cube on the right shows an optional way of indicating which components live on a particular node. You can also define your own "visual" stereotypes for nodes, as we'll see shortly.

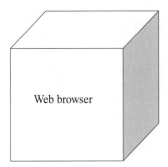 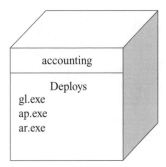

**Figure 4-8: Nodes**

A UML **deployment diagram** shows a collection of nodes, and also the dependencies and associations among those nodes. On a deployment diagram, an association between nodes represents a physical connection. It's common to see these connections labeled with various user-defined stereotypes, such as «RS-232» and «Ethernet», that indicate the nature of the connections.

Figure 4-9 shows a deployment diagram for The Internet Bookstore. This diagram shows that this set of physical elements of the bookstore system uses a variation of the standard client/server approach, with the various instances of the Web browser representing the client. In this case, the user-defined icons clearly add visual appeal and aid in understanding the diagram.

You can think of a deployment model as containing a set of what might be called deployment packages. Figure 4-10 shows some of the contents of a deployment package for our bookstore.

### Architecture Description (View of the Deployment Model)

Part of the architecture description is a view of the deployment model that contains the architecturally significant elements of that model. This generally includes the entire contents of the model.

# Workers

The following subsections describe the various workers that play key roles within the Design workflow. (Remember that in this context, a worker is a logical role, not a physical person.)

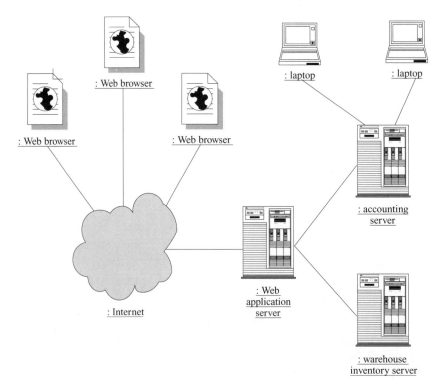

**Figure 4-9: Deployment Diagram**

## Architect

Within the Design workflow, the architect is responsible for the following:

- Outlining the design model and the deployment model, in terms of initial design subsystems, design classes, nodes, and generic mechanisms (see "Perform Architectural Design" later in this chapter)
- Ensuring the completeness and correctness of the design model and the deployment model
- Including the architecturally significant use case realizations–design and design classes, and the key aspects of the deployment model, in the architecture description (see "Architecture Description (View of the Design Model)" and "Architecture Description (View of the Deployment Model)" earlier in this chapter).

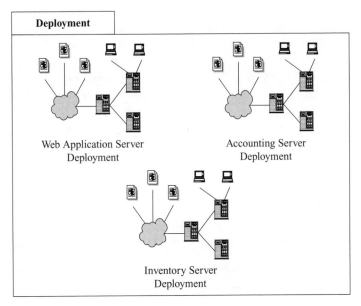

**Figure 4-10: Deployment Package**

 See "Architect" in Chapters 2 and 3 for information about other roles that the architect plays within the Unified Process.

## Use Case Engineer

Within the Design workflow, a use case engineer builds one or more use case realizations–design (see "Design a Use Case" later in this chapter). This includes defining outline versions of the design classes that come into play during these realizations.

 See "Use Case Engineer" in Chapter 3 for information about another role that the use case engineer plays within the Unified Process.

## Component Engineer

Within the Design workflow, a component engineer is responsible for the full definitions of one or more design classes and for the contents of one or more design subsystems (see "Design a Class" and "Design a Subsystem" later in this chapter). This includes ensuring that the design classes and use case realizations–design defined by the use case engineer(s) work well together. The component engineer is also responsible for defining the interfaces associated with the given design classes and design subsystems.

 See "Component Engineer" in Chapter 3 for information about other roles that the component engineer plays within the Unified Process.

# Activities

Figure 4-11 shows the various activities that workers perform within the Design workflow.

The following subsections describe these activities.

## Perform Architectural Design

This activity involves creating outlines of the deployment model and the design model. An architect (see "Architect" earlier in this chapter) is responsible for performing this activity.

The goals of outlining the deployment model include the following:

- Make initial determinations about the configuration of the physical elements of the system, including the types of nodes, the connections among them, and the necessary communication protocols.

- Commit to the distribution technologies, such as CORBA, and component technologies, such as EJBs, that the system will use.

- Start exploring the specifics of how to distribute the required functionality across the system.

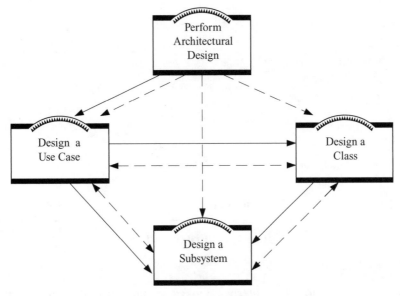

**Figure 4-11: Design Workflow Activities**

The key elements of the design model from an architectural standpoint are the design subsystems, their interfaces, and the dependencies among subsystems. These subsystems should trace directly to analysis packages (see "Analysis Package" in Chapter 3). This is also where the architect outlines subsystems that address issues such as the object request broker (ORB), database replication, and security. In addition, the architect addresses requirements associated with concurrency by identifying potential active classes (see "Design Class" earlier in this chapter).

At this point, the architect also seeks to identify generic design mechanisms that the team can later express in terms of more specific elements of the design model, such as design classes. The UML offers several ways to express these kinds of mechanisms, including the **pattern**, which the UML defines as a solution to a problem that's common to a variety of contexts, and the **framework**, which is an architectural pattern that provides a template that you can use to extend applications.

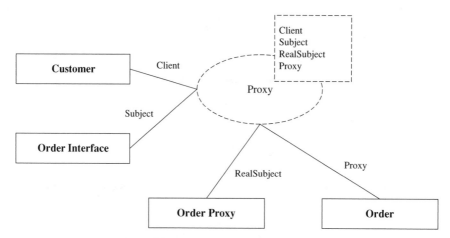

**Figure 4-12: Proxy Pattern**

Figure 4-12 shows how The Internet Bookstore makes use of a design pattern called the Proxy pattern, which is described in *Design Patterns* (Gamma, Helm, Johnson, and Vlissides; Addison-Wesley, 1995), in the context of a Customer and an Order that he or she has placed.

 See "Patterns" in Chapter 9 of *UML Explained* for more information about this use of the Proxy pattern.

Figure 4-13 shows how we use the UML to represent an architectural pattern called Model-View-Controller (MVC) using some of the key architectural features of our on-line bookstore.

## Design a Use Case

This activity involves building a use case realization–design for a use case. The resulting robustness diagram (see Figure 3-4 in Chapter 3 for an example) identifies objects that belong to design classes and the relationships among those classes.

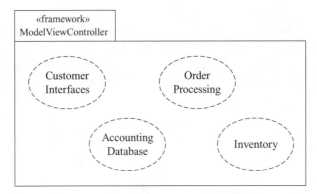

**Figure 4-13: Model-View-Controller Pattern**

A use case engineer (see "Use Case Engineer" earlier in this chapter), preferably the same one who built the corresponding use case realization–analysis, is responsible for performing this activity.

The project team may wish to supplement the sequence diagram (and collaboration diagram, if one exists) for a use case realization–design with one or more diagrams showing the design subsystems and interfaces that participate in the realization. These subsystems should trace to the analysis package that contains the use case realization–analysis associated with the given use case.

The use case engineer is also responsible for identifying special requirements relevant to the given realization.

The architect captures the architecturally interesting use case realizations–design in the architecture description (see "Architecture Description (View of the Deployment Model)" earlier in this chapter).

## Design a Class

This activity involves expanding the definition of a design class that participates in one or more use case realizations–design. Each design class should trace to one or more analysis classes (see "Analysis Class" in Chapter 3). A component engineer (see "Component Engineer" earlier in this chapter), preferably the same one who defined the corresponding analysis class(es), is responsible for performing this activity.

A design class should have a full set of operations. These operations should contain the level of detail (for instance, visibility, parameter lists, and return types) that adds value to the design model. There should be a strong correlation between the operations assigned to a class and the responsibilities of that class. This is also the appropriate place to add details to the attributes for the class, such as types and default values.

During this activity, the team also continues to refine and expand the relationships in which a design class participates. Decisions about generalization are particularly important at this stage; for instance, the component engineer is likely to move operations up and down the class hierarchy in search of the optimal places for them. Issues such as navigability across associations also become important here.

The architect captures the architecturally interesting design classes in the architecture description (see "Architecture Description (View of the Design Model)" earlier in this chapter).

## Design a Subsystem

This activity involves designing a design subsystem that was outlined during architectural design. The goal is to come up with a subsystem that provides the appropriate interfaces, and the design classes and use case realizations–design that realize the operations those interfaces offer, while the subsystem remains loosely coupled with other subsystems (that is, dependencies of this subsystem on other subsystems are minimized). A component engineer (see "Component Engineer" earlier in this chapter), preferably the same one who defined the corresponding analysis package(s), is responsible for performing this activity.

Figure 4-14 shows some of our bookstore's subsystems, and the system as a whole, using UML notation.

Note each subsystem is represented with package notation, as is the overall system. The black diamonds indicate that the subsystems have composition relationships with the system, which means that if the system is destroyed, the subsystems will be destroyed as well.

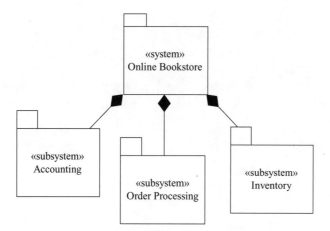

**Figure 4-14: Systems and Subsystems**

The architect captures the design subsystems in the architecture description (see "Architecture Description (View of the Design Model)" earlier in this chapter).

Chapter 5

# The Implementation Workflow

## Introduction

The fundamental goal of the **Implementation workflow** is for the development team to build a working version of the system that it can deliver to beta customers for evaluation. The primary result of this workflow is the implementation model, which contains the source code and executables that together form the implemented system. The team also expands the deployment model, which gets started during the Design phase (see "Deployment Model" in Chapter 4), to reflect the physical distribution of the various pieces of the software.

The implementation model represents the real-world realization of the contents of the design model. Each element of that model becomes part of a component, which is a physical and replaceable part of the system that conforms to, and realizes, a set of interfaces. Similarly, the full deployment model reflects the real-world realization of the architecture that has been evolving as work has proceeded on the various models.

## Artifacts

The following subsections describe the various artifacts that may be generated within the Implementation workflow.

### Component

A **component** is a physical and replaceable part of a system that conforms to, and realizes, a set of interfaces. (See "Interface" in Chapter 4 for an introduction to interfaces.)

There are some important differences between components and classes:

- A component is a *physical* thing that lives on some piece of hardware; a class is a *conceptual* thing that is physically realized within a component.

- Something talking to a component can generally access the operations it encompasses only through its interfaces, and that thing cannot access a component's attributes directly at all. A class can expose its attributes to subclasses or to everyone.

The UML assigns components to one of three categories.

- A **deployment component** is an executable part of a system. The UML defines two stereotypes for use on deployment components: *«executable»*, which usually indicates a binary (EXE) file, and *«library»*, which indicates a static or dynamic object library such as a DLL.

- A **work product component** is a component that's part of the system but isn't executable. There are three UML-defined stereotypes for work product components: *«table»* (for a database table), *«file»* (for a file that contains source code), and *«document»*. Within the Unified Process, «file» components package design classes (see "Design Class" in Chapter 4) and their interfaces.

- An **execution component** is created as a result of an executing system. One kind of execution component is a COM+ object, which a system creates as an instantiation of a DLL at runtime.

A **component diagram** shows a collection of related components. You might think of a component diagram as a type of class diagram that shows components instead of classes. This kind of diagram can show the various kinds of relationships that components can have, which are the same as the ones classes can have. Generally, though, the focus will be on the interfaces that components expose and use, and the dependencies that exist among the various components. (Dependency arrows on a component diagram show how each component uses interfaces exposed by other components.)

Figure 5-1 shows a component diagram for our bookstore that uses the standard UML notation for components.

 See "Component Diagrams" in Chapter 10 of *UML Explained* for more about component diagrams.

## Interface

The two notations for the relationships between components and interfaces are the same as those for classes (see "Interface" in Chapter 4) and interfaces.

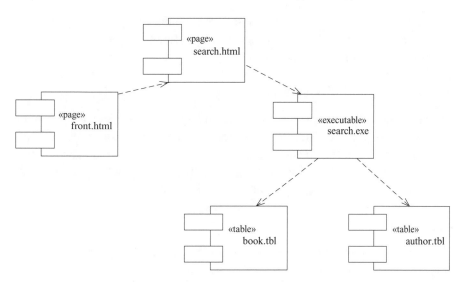

**Figure 5-1: Component Diagram**

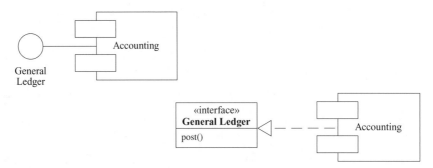

**Figure 5-2: Component and Component Interface**

Lollipop notation shows the interface as a circle attached to a component with a straight line. The other notation involves defining the interface as a stereo-typed class and drawing a dashed line from the component to the interface, with an open triangle at the end with the interface.

Figure 5-2 shows both notations for a component and a related interface that belong to The Internet Bookstore.

The collection of interfaces associated with a component or an implementation subsystem must reflect all of the services offered by the elements of that component or subsystem.

## Implementation Subsystem

An **implementation subsystem** is a UML package that contains components, as well as interfaces connected to components and the subsystem itself. An implementation subsystem can also contain other implementation subsystems. A given implementation subsystem should trace directly to one or more design subsystems (see "Design Subsystem" in Chapter 4).

## Implementation Model

The **implementation model** is basically a package of what might be called implementation packages. This model can be considered correct when it contains all of the components and implementation subsystems required to realize the functionality specified by the use cases contained within the use case model (see "User-Interface Prototype" in Chapter 2), the contents of the design model (see "Design Model" in Chapter 4), and the supplementary requirements (see "Supplementary Requirements" in Chapter 2).

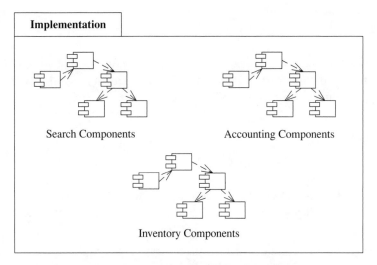

**Figure 5-3: Implementation Package**

Figure 5-3 shows some of the contents of an implementation package for our bookstore.

## Architecture Description (View of the Implementation Model)

Part of the architecture description is a view of the implementation model that contains the architecturally significant elements of that model. This generally includes:

- The implementation subsystems, including their interfaces, and the relationships among the subsystems
- The key components, including «executable» components and those «file» components that package architecturally significant design classes

## Integration Build Plan

The **integration build plan** describes the builds that will occur within a given iteration. This description includes, for each build, the functionality that the build will likely implement (in terms of use cases) and the parts of the implementation model affected by the build (in terms of components and implementation subsystems).

## Workers

The following subsections describe the various workers that play key roles within the Implementation workflow. (Remember that in this context, a worker is a logical role, not a physical person.)

### Architect

Within the Implementation workflow, the architect is responsible for:

- Outlining the implementation model, in terms of initial «executable» components (see "Perform Architectural Implementation" later in this chapter)
- Ensuring the completeness and correctness of the implementation model
- Mapping the executable components onto nodes within the deployment model
- Including the components from the implementation model, and the updated contents of the deployment model, in the architecture description (see "Architecture Description (View of the Implementation Model)," earlier in this chapter, and "Architecture Description (View of the Deployment Model)," in Chapter 4)

See "Architect" in Chapters 2, 3, and 4 for information about other roles that the architect plays within the Unified Process.

### Component Engineer

Within the Implementation workflow, a component engineer is responsible for the source code of one or more «file» components and for the contents of one or more implementation subsystems (see "Implement a Class" and "Implement a Subsystem" later in this chapter), and for the interfaces associated with those components and subsystems. The component engineer is also responsible for unit testing of his or her components (see "Perform Unit Test" later in this chapter).

See "Component Engineer" in Chapters 3 and 4 for information about other roles that the component engineer plays within the Unified Process.

### System Integrator

The **system integrator** is responsible for designing the integration build plan and performing incremental integration of builds (see "Integrate the System" later in this chapter).

## Activities

Figure 5-4 shows the various activities that workers perform within the Implementation workflow.

The following subsections describe these activities.

### Perform Architectural Implementation

This activity involves identifying the architecturally significant components for the given iteration and mapping the associated executable components onto nodes. An architect (see "Architect" earlier in this chapter) is responsible for performing this activity. The components become part of the implementation model; the mapping of components to nodes becomes part of the architecture description.

The architect captures the architecturally interesting components in the architecture description (see "Architecture Description (View of the Implementation Model)" earlier in this chapter).

### Implement a Class

This activity involves expanding the definition of a design class and building a «file» component, or expanding an existing «file» component, to contain the class. This includes generating code, in the form of methods, for the operations that the design class specifies, as well as for the various relationships in which that class is involved.

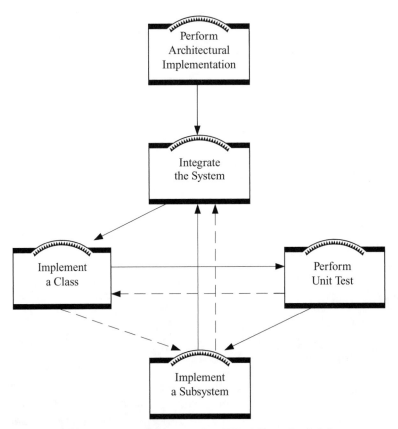

**Figure 5-4: Implementation Workflow Activities**

The component to which the implementation class belongs must also support the same interfaces as the design class(es) it implements. A component engineer (see "Component Engineer" earlier in this chapter), preferably the same one who built the corresponding design class, is responsible for performing this activity.

## Perform Unit Test

This activity involves producing executable code from a «file» component, and then performing specification tests and structural tests on that code independent of other components. A component engineer (see "Component Engineer" earlier in this chapter) is responsible for performing this activity.

**Specification testing**, also known as **black-box testing** or **responsibility-based testing**, tries to verify the behavior of a given component without considering what's inside the component. This kind of testing occurs on class methods, classes as units, and components as units. One way of performing this kind of testing on a method involves the following steps:

1. Identify the testable functions that the method performs. (It's likely that a method, even a small one, performs more than one discrete function.)

2. Identify the input and output values of each of those functions.

3. Put the input values into categories such that each value belongs to only one category. (The concept of a category is roughly equivalent to that of the equivalence class.)

4. Partition each category into specific test values (for instance, a set of values squarely in the range, some values near the upper and lower bounds of the range, and some illegal values).

5. Identify constraints on those values (in other words, identify choices to exclude; reasons to exclude values include performance constraints).

6. Generate one test case for all combinations of choices.

7. Develop expected results for each test case, based on trusted sources such as a program specification and developer knowledge.

**Structural testing**, also known as **white-box testing** or **implementation-based testing**, tries to verify the internal workings of the code inside a method, class, or component. Formal testing of this kind often makes use of a **control flow graph**, which shows which chunks of code can be followed by which other chunks. One variation of this is called a **method flow graph**; this graph shows how an object reaches various states in response to what's going on inside of a method execution. A designer can substitute a method flow graph into a state diagram (see Figure 4-2) to see the complete picture from a code analysis standpoint. A **class flow graph** is a combination of method flow graphs that models all control flow paths through the class as a unit.

See Robert Binder's *Testing Object-Oriented Systems: Models, Patterns, and Tools* (Addison-Wesley, 2000) for more information about responsibility-based testing and implementation-based testing.

## Implement a Subsystem

This activity involves building an implementation subsystem that was outlined during architectural implementation. The goal is to come up with a subsystem that provides interfaces that match up with those in the corresponding design subsystem(s) (see "Design Subsystem" in Chapter 4) and components that implement design classes, while the subsystem remains loosely coupled with other subsystems (which means that dependencies of this subsystem on other subsystems are minimized). A component engineer (see "Component Engineer" earlier in this chapter), preferably the same one who built the corresponding design subsystem(s), is responsible for performing this activity.

The architect captures the implementation subsystems in the architecture description (see "Architecture Description (View of the Implementation Model)" earlier in this chapter).

## Integrate the System

This activity involves creating or expanding upon the integration build plan so that it reflects the contents of the next build of the system, and integrating the various pieces of that build (which are based on some or all of the implementation subsystems and components) before integration testing begins. The premise of incremental development is that the new build will add functionality to the current build and also address defects in that build. A system integrator (see "System Integrator" earlier in this chapter) is responsible for performing this activity.

Chapter 6

# The Test Workflow

## Introduction

The fundamental goal of the **Test workflow** is for the project team to ensure that the system offers a high degree of quality before it's delivered to customers. The primary result of this workflow is the test model, which contains the various inputs to testing, in the form of plans, cases, and procedures, and also the outputs, defects, and evaluations.

## Artifacts

The following subsections describe the various artifacts that may be generated within the Test workflow.

### Test Case

A **test case** specifies how you should test part of a system. This specification includes the inputs, the expected outputs, and the conditions under which the test should occur.

Black-box testing within the Unified Process involves test cases derived directly from use cases (see "Use Case" in Chapter 2). White-box testing involves test cases derived from use case realizations–design (see "Use Case

Realization–Design" in Chapter 3). Other kinds of test cases include those for integration testing (see "Perform Integration Test" later this chapter) and those that operate on the system level (see "Perform System Test" later in this chapter). These test cases address subjects such as "negative" testing (trying to break the system) and stress testing (trying to overload system resources).

## Test Procedure

A **test procedure** specifies how to perform all or parts of one or more test cases. As you might expect, a test procedure associated with black-box testing will follow the various paths specified by the flows of events of the given use case, whereas a white-box test procedure will follow the sequence indicated by the sequence diagram for the given use case realization–design.

## Test Component

A **test component** is a piece of code that automates all or parts of one or more test procedures. (Other terms for test component include test harness and test script.) A component engineer usually develops test components either by writing them in a scripting language (such as Perl) or a regular programming language (for example, C++), or by capturing tester actions and system responses using some kind of test automation tool.

## Test Model

The **test model** is a UML package that contains the test cases, test procedures, and test components for the system being built.

## Test Plan

The **test plan** describes the resources that will be available for testing and the schedule of tests, as well as the test strategy, which specifies what tests will be performed within each iteration, and things like required levels of code coverage.

## Defect

The term **defect** refers to any problem with the system that developers need to track and resolve.

### Test Evaluation

A **test evaluation** is an evaluation of the results of a set of tests. A test evaluation generally includes a list of defects and their priority levels, and also information such as the ratio of defects to lines of code.

## Workers

The following subsections describe the various workers that play key roles within the Test workflow. (Remember that in this context, a worker is a logical role, not a physical person.)

### Test Engineer

The test engineer is responsible for:

- Planning integration, system, and regression testing (see "Plan Test" later in this chapter)
- Selecting and describing test cases and corresponding test procedures (see "Design Test" later in this chapter)
- Ensuring the completeness and correctness of the test model
- Evaluating the results of testing (see "Evaluate Test" later in this chapter)

### Component Engineer

Within the Test workflow, a component engineer is responsible for building one or more test components (see "Implement Test" later in this chapter).

 See "Component Engineer" in Chapters 4 and 5 for information about other roles that the component engineer plays within the Unified Process.

### Integration Tester

An integration tester is responsible for performing integration testing on each build of the system (see "Perform Integration Test" later in this chapter).

## System Tester

A system tester is responsible for performing system testing on each build of the system (see "Perform System Test" later in this chapter).

# Activities

Figure 6-1 shows the various activities that workers perform within the Test workflow. The following subsections describe these activities.

## Plan Test

This activity involves developing a test plan for the given iteration. A test engineer (see "Test Engineer" earlier in this chapter) is responsible for performing this activity.

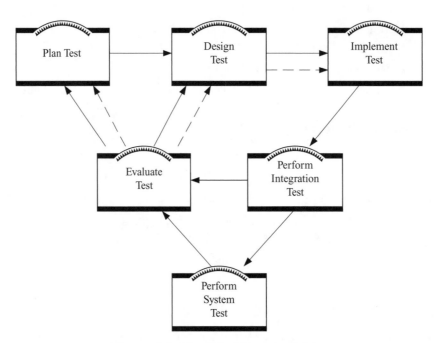

**Figure 6-1: Test Workflow Activities**

Since it's impossible to ever completely test a system of any meaningful size, doing test planning generally involves identifying test cases, test procedures, and test components that will offer the best return on investment in terms of improved system quality. The focus should be on testing the most important use cases and those nonfunctional requirements associated with the highest risks.

There are two basic test strategies that a QA team can employ:

- Focus on feature sufficiency, which involves **conformance-directed testing**, whose goals involve executing tests designed to establish conformance to customer requirements.

- Focus on fault efficiency, which involves **fault-directed testing**, whose goals involve executing tests designed to have a high probability of revealing faults.

## Design Test

This activity involves designing the various levels of tests that QA people need to perform on each build of the evolving system, and also the procedures they'll follow to carry out those tests. A test engineer (see "Test Engineer" earlier in this chapter) is responsible for performing this activity.

- Integration testing involves exercising the interfaces between components to demonstrate that those components work well together. Integration test cases can be based directly on use case realizations–design (see "Use Case Realization–Design" in Chapter 4).

- System test cases should involve combinations of related use cases that tend to be performed in parallel and that involve extensive chunks of the system. System testing focuses on conformance to functional requirements and also nonfunctional requirements such as those dealing with performance and stress/load.

- The test engineer(s) should design integration and system test cases with an eye toward reuse within regression testing wherever possible. Regression testing tends to focus on retesting changed code or the implementations of particularly risky use cases.

- Reuse of test cases within test procedures, and of the procedures themselves, should also be a high priority within this activity.

All of the test cases go into the test model.

### Implement Test

This activity involves creating test components that automate test procedures, by using a test automation tool, programming the components, or both. A component engineer (see "Component Engineer" earlier in this chapter) is responsible for performing this activity. All of the test components go into the test model.

### Perform Integration Test

This activity involves performing manual and automated integration testing for each build of the system. The integration testers (see "Integration Tester" earlier in this chapter) report defects to the component engineers or test engineers as appropriate.

### Perform System Test

This activity involves performing manual and automated system testing for each build of the system. A system tester (see "System Tester" earlier in this chapter) is responsible for performing this activity. A good rule of thumb is that system testing should start when the results of integration testing satisfy the quality goals specified in the test plan.

### Evaluate Test

This activity involves evaluating the results of integration and system testing for a given iteration, by comparing those results to the appropriate quality goals described in the test plan. A test engineer (see "Test Engineer" earlier in this chapter) is responsible for performing this activity.

The key measure is that of reliability; measuring the completeness of testing, or **coverage**, is usually also very important. Generally, the project manager determines the acceptable level of coverage. One way the QA team can accomplish this involves the following steps:

1. Perform some testing to establish that the system is at least minimally operational.
2. Execute the full test suite and evaluate the results of each test.
3. Use a coverage tool to calibrate the system.
4. Run the full suite again, but this time, focus on the coverage level.

5.  As necessary, develop more tests to exercise code that hasn't been covered, and add these to the suite.

6.  Stop testing when the coverage goal is met and all tests pass.

The test evaluation also includes recommendations as to how to proceed from a QA standpoint. For example, the test engineers may specify additional testing or suggest that certain tests be less rigorous. Alternatively, it may be desirable to redefine the increment associated with the given iteration so it includes only those parts of the system that passed integration and system testing.

# Chapter 7

# The Inception Phase

## Introduction

The primary goal of the Inception phase is to establish the business case for the proposed system. The initial version of the business case is the justification for committing to the development project; later versions are meant to justify the continued existence of the project. The key steps involved in reaching this goal include the following:

- Establish the scope of the system. All the stakeholders must agree in principle on what the system will contain and how it will interact with its external environment.

- Explore the high-level functional and nonfunctional requirements. Do some use case modeling to capture the most significant requirements that will serve to start driving development.

- Put together a **candidate architecture**, which is a bare-bones architecture composed of initial versions of the six basic models. Ensure that the stakeholders buy into this architecture as a viable foundation on which the system can be built.

- Identify the most critical risks that the project will face, those that affect the feasibility of the project, and specify how the project team will deal with them.

- Specify some values, such as return on investment (ROI) or productivity gains, that will indicate reasons to do the project from an economic/financial standpoint.

The effort put forth during Inception might involve one person drawing a few diagrams and putting together rudimentary documentation, or it might involve a team of people performing a significant amount of research; most likely, it will lie between these extremes. In any case, Inception is not meant to be a terribly time-consuming and expensive exercise. The idea is to do enough digging into the ideas behind the proposed system to find out whether it makes sense to start building it.

The following list offers an overview of how the five workflows (see Chapters 2 through 6) cut across the Inception phase.

- **Requirements**: This workflow receives most of the attention during Inception. There are four key tasks to perform as part of this workflow:
  - Build the feature list for the system.
  - Reach agreement among the stakeholders about the system context, as expressed in a high-level domain model (and, optionally, a business model).
  - Capture the high-level functional requirements in the form of use cases.
  - Start capturing major nonfunctional requirements.

> **DELIVERABLE**   The feature list is a deliverable of the Inception phase.

- **Analysis**: The key task to perform as part of this workflow during Inception is to build an initial version of the analysis model based on the initial set of use cases.
- **Design**: The key Design task to perform during Inception is to build initial versions of the deployment model and the design model.
- **Implementation**: It's generally not necessary to address Implementation activities during Inception, unless some kind of working prototype needs to be built to address customer concerns.

- **Test**: This workflow is only relevant to Inception if there's a prototype in place and it looks likely that it will be something that the team can build on as development progresses.

## Getting Started

The following subsections describe the tasks that the project manager should perform before the development team begins the activities specified by the five workflows.

### Plan the Inception Phase

The objective of this task is to produce an initial project plan that describes, in some detail, how work will proceed in this phase, and, in more abstract terms, how work would proceed through the other phases. The detail for the phase should include overall budget and schedule for one iteration (perhaps two, if necessary, but there shouldn't be more than two iterations for Inception). The rough phase plan for the proposed Elaboration, Construction, and Transition phases should reflect first-cut guesses at the number of iterations and associated budget, schedule, and staffing numbers.

 **DELIVERABLE** The initial version of the project plan is a deliverable of the Inception phase.

### Expand the System Vision

Every project has some kind of vision statement at the beginning. Unfortunately, many times the statement is mostly in someone's head, and even if it's written down, the vision tends to be very vague, open-ended, unrealistic, or all of these. The next task of the project manager during Inception is to build a vision statement that all the stakeholders can understand and agree on. This statement outlines the very high-level requirements of the proposed system and the expectations to be placed on the project team, as well as a preliminary assessment of the risks that the project will face. A proper vision statement serves as a solid foundation for the development of the business case, which is discussed later in this chapter.

## Establish the Evaluation Criteria

The key criteria that the project team need to meet during Inception can usefully be classified into five areas.

- **Scope**: All of the stakeholders agree, on an initial basis, on what's "in" and what's "out." There's enough information in the vision statement to ensure that what's "in" will form a working system. The specification of what's "out" includes all of the key actors and some kind of indication of the nature of what the interfaces will be between those actors and the system.

- **High-level requirements**: The high-level requirements, expressed in the form of use cases that drive the project team's initial exploration of the system's behavior and structure, are unambiguous and free of redundancies and contradictions, and taken together are sufficient to serve as the foundation for ongoing expansion and negotiation of requirements at lower levels of detail.

- **Candidate architecture**: A candidate architecture that appears to meet the needs of the users is in place. It promises to make good use of the technologies that the team will use to build the system; run effectively and efficiently; and earn good marks for the "-ilities" (reliability, maintainability, and so forth). It also lends itself well to evolution as requirements grow.

- **Critical risks**: All of the critical risks—the ones that clearly threaten the success of the project—have been identified, and it's been specified how the team will mitigate each of them (for instance, by reducing the probability that a given risk will occur, or by having an alternate plan in case bringing in a particular piece of technology causes more problems than it solves).

 The initial risk list is a deliverable of the Inception phase.

- **Initial business case**: The initial business case (see "Make the Initial Business Case" later in this chapter) is sound enough, conceptually and financially, to justify the decision to proceed with Elaboration.

## Requirements Activities

The following subsections describe the Requirements workflow activities that are of interest during the Inception phase.

### Build the Domain Model

The primary goal of domain modeling during this phase is to help the stake-holders reach agreement on the overall context of the system—in other words, what's in and what's out. The result should be one or two high-level class diagrams that capture the major classes that will serve as a good starting point, and a foundation, for further exploration of the static structure of the system.

> **DELIVERABLE** The initial version of the domain model is a deliverable of the Inception phase.

During Iteration 1, the team developing The Internet Bookstore identified 10 high-level classes on which to focus. Figure 7-1 shows what the domain-level class diagram looks like after this iteration.

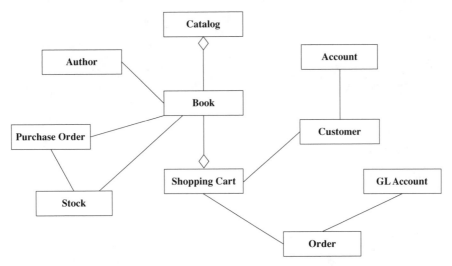

**Figure 7-1: Class Diagram After Iteration 1**

## Build the Business Model

The primary goal of business modeling during Inception is to help the project team identify major actors and use cases, and also get an overview of the high-level business processes that the team will be modeling.

 The initial version is a deliverable of the Inception phase.

## Find Actors and Use Cases

During Inception, the team focuses on finding those use cases that will help the architect envision the candidate architecture, and those actors that play roles in conjunction with those use cases. These actors and use cases become the initial contents of the use case model.

 The initial version of the use case model is a deliverable of the Inception phase.

The architect adds the initial version of the use case model to the candidate architecture description.

 The description of the candidate architecture is a deliverable of the Inception phase.

During Iteration 1, the team developing The Internet Bookstore identified five actors and 13 use cases. The actors included the following:

- Accountant
- Accounting Clerk
- Customer
- Inventory Clerk
- Order Fulfiller

The use cases included the following:

- Add Book to Shopping Cart
- Check Out
- Create Account
- Fulfill Order
- Log In
- Maintain Account
- Post to GL
- Print GL Report
- Reorder Books
- Search by Author
- Search by Title
- Set Up GL
- Ship Order

## Prioritize the Use Cases

The next task is to decide which of the use cases it's necessary to explore further during this phase. These will generally be the ones that address the most critical high-level functionality of the system and the most significant risks. This chunk of use cases will typically represent no more than 5 or 10 percent of what the use case model will eventually contain. The use cases that fulfill these criteria become the initial contents of the architecture description (see "Architecture Description (View of the Use Case Model)" in Chapter 2).

 The initial use case ranking list is a deliverable of the **DELIVERABLE** Inception phase.

Figure 7-2 shows the use cases that the team building The Internet Bookstore decided to focus on during Inception.

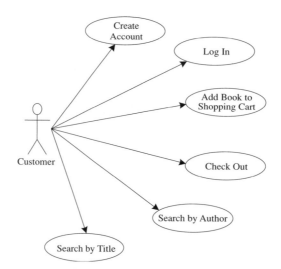

**Figure 7-2: Use Cases to Focus on During Iteration 1**

## Detail a Use Case

The final Requirements task within Inception involves writing at least some initial text for those use cases that have the highest priority. The focus will generally be on basic courses of action (see "Use Case" in Chapter 2) during this phase. A use case specifier (see "Use Case Specifier" in Chapter 2) performs this activity.

The following text describes the basic course of action of the Check Out use case that the team building The Internet Bookstore wrote during Iteration 1.

> The system retrieves the shipping addresses associated with the Customer's Account, and displays these addresses. The Customer selects an address. Then the system displays the available shipping methods on a new page. The Customer selects a shipping method. Then the system retrieves and displays billing information associated with the Customer's Account, on a third page. The Customer selects a billing method. The system displays an order confirmation page.

> The Customer confirms the order. The system creates an Order with all of the required information, and then returns the Customer to the main page.

## Analysis Activities

The following subsections describe the Analysis workflow activities that are of interest in the Inception phase.

### Perform Architectural Analysis

The architect builds a simple version of the analysis model that serves as the framework for analyzing the architecturally significant use cases.

 **DELIVERABLE**  The initial version of the analysis model is a deliverable of the Inception phase.

The architect adds the initial version of the analysis model to the architecture description.

Figure 7-3 shows the analysis model that resulted from the work that the team building The Internet Bookstore did during Inception.

### Analyze a Use Case

During Inception, the team should analyze only those use cases that will help the architect define the candidate architecture.

The team building The Internet Bookstore performed robustness analysis for the four use cases identified during the Prioritize the Use Cases activity. Figure 7-4 shows the results of their analysis of the Check Out use case.

The team added the boundary objects to a new class diagram, and also added the new Shipping Method class to the class diagram for the domain model.

## Design Activities

The following subsections describe the Design workflow activities that are of interest in the Inception phase.

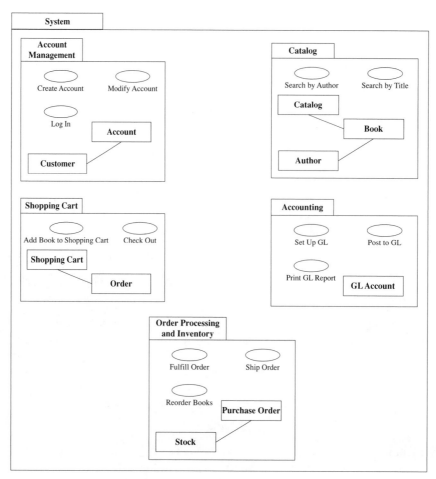

**Figure 7-3: Analysis Model After Iteration 1**

## Perform Architectural Design

The architect builds simple versions of the deployment model and the design model that together serve as a framework for exploring the design of the system in later phases of the project.

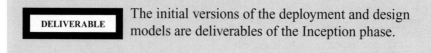

**DELIVERABLE** The initial versions of the deployment and design models are deliverables of the Inception phase.

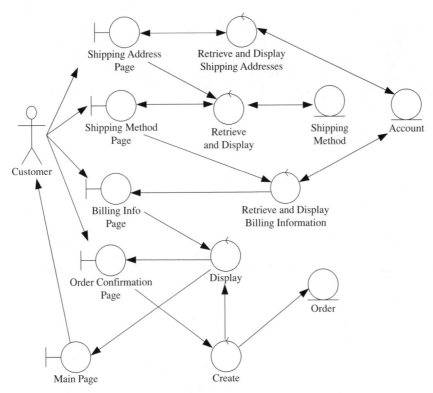

**Figure 7-4: Robustness Diagram for Check Out Use Case**

The architect adds the initial versions of the deployment model and the design model to the candidate architecture description.

Figure 4-9 is one of the deployment diagrams that the team building The Internet Bookstore drew during the Inception iteration. Figure 7-5 is their initial representation of the design model.

## Taking Stock

The following subsections describe what the team should do at the end of each iteration within the Inception phase and at the end of the entire phase.

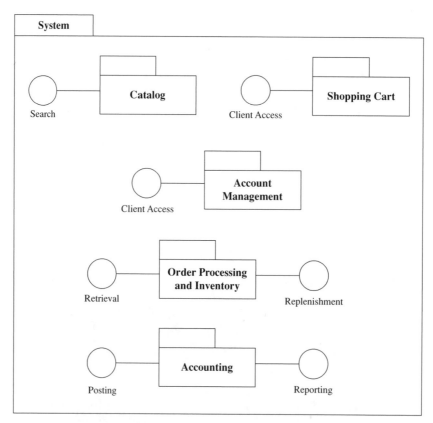

**Figure 7-5: Design Model After Iteration 1**

## Assess Each Iteration

Generally, a team doesn't do more than one iteration within the Inception phase, but it may become a good idea under some circumstances. For instance, if during the first iteration, the need for a user-interface prototype appears, or there's a sense that not all of the most important risks have been identified and addressed, the project manager might call for a second iteration. (It's highly unlikely that a third iteration would be necessary, though, because that would likely indicate at least one excellent reason not to pursue the project.)

## Assess the Phase as a Whole

Here are some key questions to ask at the end of the Inception phase before work on the project proceeds:

- Is it clear to all of the stakeholders what's going to be inside of the new system and what's going to be outside?
- Does everyone understand and agree upon the high-level requirements?
- Is there a reasonably good candidate architecture?
- Have the critical risks been identified, and are plans in place for addressing them?
- Does it make economic and business sense to proceed with the project?

If the answers to these questions are positive in the eyes of at least the majority of stakeholders, then the project should be a go. If not, then a no-go decision, or a decision to do some rethinking and rework, is probably the best choice.

# Looking Ahead

The following subsections describe the tasks that the project manager should perform before the project proceeds to Elaboration.

## Make the Initial Business Case

If the stakeholders all agree that the results of Inception indicate the project should proceed to Elaboration, the team needs to expand the vision document to create the **business case**, which is the justification for the system expressed in economic terms such as revenue projections and ROI.

The initial business case needs to meet only one criterion: It is compelling enough to justify the project moving into Elaboration. As such, the project manager should leverage what the development team knows at this point to the greatest extent possible, but he or she should also make it clear to the other stakeholders that the financial estimates are quite rough, since they're based on a relatively small knowledge base, and that the conceptual vision presented by the business case is likely to be shortsighted in scope and low on specifics.

 **DELIVERABLE** The initial version of the business case is a deliverable of the Inception phase.

## Do Initial Planning for the Elaboration Phase

The project manager needs to establish some high-level objectives for Elaboration at this point, including:

- Finish the domain model and the business model.
- Identify a large majority of the use cases that will address the functional requirements on the system.
- Drive the architecturally significant use cases at least through design, with the idea of producing an executable architectural baseline.
- Determine how many iterations the team should make during Elaboration.
- Estimate budget, schedule, and staffing requirements based on current knowledge and educated guesses.

The next chapter discusses planning for Elaboration in more detail.

# Chapter 8

# The Elaboration Phase

## Introduction

The primary goals of the Elaboration phase are to capture a majority of the remaining functional requirements and to establish a solid architectural baseline on which further development can build. The project team also needs to expand and refine the business case for the system and address issues involving budget and schedule. The key steps involved in reaching this goal include the following:

- Develop use cases that address most of the functional requirements that weren't dealt with during Iteration.

- Create the baseline of an architecture that includes all of the architecturally significant elements of the system, which includes the key aspects of all six models, a description of the architecture as a whole, and the executable aspects of the architecture.

- Shift the focus on risk from the *critical* risks, which should have been addressed before Elaboration, to the *significant* risks, which are those that could cause meaningful schedule slips and budget overruns.

- Specify the quality levels that the system should meet with regard to nonfunctional requirements such as reliability and response times.

- Flesh out the business case and the project plan using the knowledge that the team gains during Elaboration about schedule and cost.

The effort put forth during Elaboration should be based on the nature of the most significant risks. For example, if the technical risks are fairly high, the focus is likely to be on the architecture, and that will drive development more than the use cases. On the other hand, if the requirements risk calls for extra attention throughout the phase, the focus will be on extensive exploration and negotiation of requirements, involving several passes at use case text and a lot of prototyping, and the use cases will drive development to a greater text than the architecture does.

The following list offers an overview of how the five workflows (see Chapters 2 through 6) cut across the Elaboration phase.

- **Requirements**: The team focuses on capturing a significant majority of the functional requirements, in the form of use cases, during Elaboration.

- **Analysis**: Most of the Analysis work happens during Elaboration. It's here that the team tightens up the use cases, which increases developer understanding of the functional requirements, and builds the model that leads the movement toward a structure that the team can use to build momentum as it heads into design.

- **Design**: This workflow is the other centerpiece of Elaboration, along with Analysis. The team translates the still-conceptual use case realizations–analysis, analysis classes, and analysis packages into more physical model elements that shape the system.

- **Implementation**: The goal of performing Implementation activities during Elaboration is to come up with one or more versions of an executable architectural baseline, small, skinny versions of the system that demonstrate the key features.

> **DELIVERABLE**    An executable architectural baseline is a deliverable of each iteration within the Elaboration phase.

- **Test**: The team performs integration and system testing using the executable components they built during Implementation, to establish the correctness of the functionality and also to address issues such as performance.

# Getting Started

The following subsections describe the tasks that the project manager should perform before the development team begins the activities specified by the five workflows.

## Plan the Elaboration Phase

The objective of this task is to update the project plan to include a detailed description of how work in this phase will proceed, as well as to update and expand upon the more abstract description of how work would proceed through the other phases. The detail for the phase should include specific budget and schedule numbers for each iteration. The rough phase plan for the proposed Construction and Transition phases should reflect first-cut guesses at the number of iterations and associated budget, schedule, and staffing numbers.

 An updated version of the project plan is a deliverable of the Elaboration phase.

## Establish the Evaluation Criteria

The key criteria that the project team needs to meet during Elaboration can usefully be classified into four areas.

- **Requirements**: The requirements, expressed in the form of use cases, are unambiguous and free of redundancies and contradictions. Taken together, they serve as a solid foundation for the baseline architecture, address the significant risks, and support the business case.
- **Baseline architecture**: An executable architectural baseline that has demonstrated that it meets the needs of the users is in place. It is robust enough to build upon during the Construction phase, and it is also able to withstand expansion as new requirements are placed on the system.
- **Significant risks**: All of the critical risks—the ones that clearly threaten the success of the project—have been mitigated. The significant but not critical risks have been identified, and it's been specified how the team will address each of them.

> **DELIVERABLE**    An updated risk list is a deliverable of the Elaboration phase.

- **Business case**: The business case (see "Do Initial Planning for the Construction Phase" later in this chapter) is sound enough, conceptually and financially, to justify the decision to proceed with Construction.

## Requirements Activities

The following subsections describe the Requirements workflow activities that are of interest during the Elaboration phase.

### Build the Domain Model

The project team should strive, during Elaboration, to complete the domain model, which it started as part of Inception (see "Build the Domain Model" in Chapter 7). The goals of domain modeling are defined in the section "Build the Domain Model" in Chapter 2.

> **DELIVERABLE**    The domain model is a deliverable of each iteration within the Elaboration phase.

Here's some of what resulted from this activity during the three Elaboration iterations that the team building The Internet Bookstore performed:

- **Iteration 2**: The team added Category, and aggregated Book to this new class instead of Catalog, and also added the association class BookAndAuthor.

- **Iteration 3**: The team broke out some of what they initially expected would be part of the Account class into two new classes, Billing Info and Shipping Info.

- **Iteration 4**: The team added Order History, to keep track of a Customer's Orders over time, and Shipment, in response to the initial exploration of the Process Received Shipment use case in Iteration 3 (see "Find Actors and Use Cases" later in this chapter).

Figure 8-1 shows what one of the domain-level class diagrams for the project looks like after these iterations.

## Build the Business Model

The project team should strive to complete the business model, which it started as part of Inception (see "Build the Business Model" in Chapter 7), during Elaboration. The goals of business modeling are defined in "Build the Business Model" in Chapter 2.

> **DELIVERABLE** The business model is a deliverable of each iteration within the Elaboration phase.

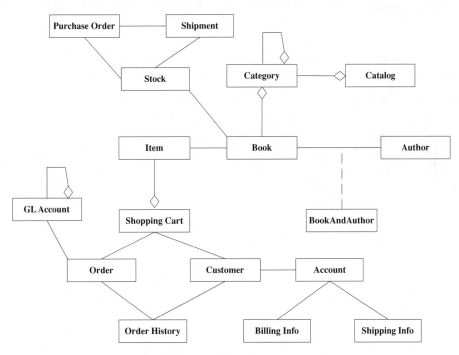

**Figure 8-1: Domain-Level Class Diagram After Iteration 4**

## Find Actors and Use Cases

The team should discover a healthy majority of the actors and use cases for the use case model (see "User-Interface Prototype" in Chapter 2) during this phase.

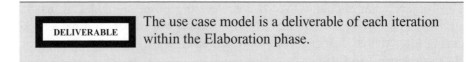

**DELIVERABLE** The use case model is a deliverable of each iteration within the Elaboration phase.

The architect adds the architecturally significant use cases to the architecture description.

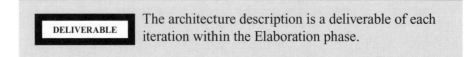

**DELIVERABLE** The architecture description is a deliverable of each iteration within the Elaboration phase.

Here's some of what resulted from this activity during the three Elaboration iterations that the team building The Internet Bookstore performed:

- **Iteration 2**: The team discovered the use cases Edit Contents of Shopping Cart and Search by Category, both performed by the Customer actor, and added them to the Shopping Cart and Catalog packages, respectively.

- **Iteration 3**: The team discovered the use case Process Received Shipment, performed by the Inventory Clerk actor, and added it to the Inventory package. (See "Analyze a Package" later in this chapter to learn about how Order Processing and Inventory became separate packages during Iteration 3.)

- **Iteration 4**: The team discovered the use cases Suspend and Reactivate Account, performed by the Account Administrator actor, and Update Customer History, performed by the Marketing Representative actor, and added these use cases and actors to the Account Management package.

Figure 8-2 shows these new use cases.

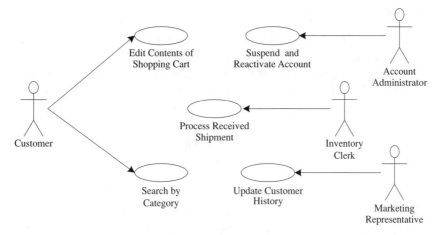

**Figure 8-2: New Use Cases After Iteration 4**

## Prototype the User Interface

Within Elaboration, this activity focuses on designing the look and feel of those parts of the user interface that address the architecturally significant use cases (see "Architecture Description (View of the Use Case Model)" in Chapter 2).

Here's some of what resulted from this activity during the three Elaboration iterations that the team building The Internet Bookstore performed:

- **Iteration 2**: The team built prototypes that correspond with the Shopping Cart use cases Add Book to Shopping Cart and Check Out, and for the Category use cases Search by Author and Search by Title.

- **Iteration 3**: The team built prototypes for the Account Management use cases Create Account, Log In, and Maintain Account, and expanded on the prototypes they built in Iteration 2 to address the use cases Edit Contents of Shopping Cart and Search by Category, which they started exploring in Iteration 2 (see "Find Actors and Use Cases" on the previous page).

- **Iteration 4**: The team built prototypes for the Order Processing use cases Fulfill Order and Ship Order, and the Accounting use cases Set Up GL, Post to GL, and Print GL Report.

## Prioritize the Use Cases

The next task is to decide which use cases in the now fairly complete use case model to explore during which Elaboration phase iteration. As you might expect by now, those use cases that describe important functionality and address significant risks should receive priority. This chunk of use cases will likely represent the major part of the use case model (perhaps as much as 80 percent). These use cases go into the architecture description (see "Architecture Description (View of the Use Case Model)" in Chapter 2); they also serve as a key driver of the integration build plan (see "Integration Build Plan" in Chapter 5).

The team building The Internet Bookstore made these decisions:

- **Iteration 2**: Perform robustness analysis on the Shopping Cart and Catalog use cases; write initial text for the Account Management use cases.

- **Iteration 3**: Design the Shopping Cart use cases; perform robustness analysis on the Account Management use cases; write initial text for the Order Processing, Inventory, and Accounting use cases.

- **Iteration 4**: Implement the Shopping Cart use cases; design and implement the Catalog use cases; perform robustness analysis on the Order Processing, Inventory, and Accounting use cases; design the Order Processing use cases.

## Detail a Use Case

The team writes detailed text, for the basic course and all alternate courses (see "Use Case" in Chapter 2), for all of the use cases being addressed within the given iteration. The user-interface prototypes (see "Prototype the User Interface" earlier in this chapter) should serve as an excellent source of text for basic courses of action; the project team must take care, however, to pay particular attention to alternate courses that aren't represented within the prototype. (As a reminder, alternate courses typically address error conditions and infrequently taken paths.)

The following text describes the basic and alternate courses of action of the Edit Contents of Shopping Cart use case that the team building The Internet Bookstore wrote during Iteration 3.

*Main flow of events:* On the Shopping Cart Page, the Customer modifies the quantity of an Item in the Shopping Cart, and then presses the Update button. The system stores the new quantity, and then computes and displays the new cost for that Item.

The Customer presses the Continue Shopping button. The system returns control to the use case from which it received control.

*Exceptional flow of events:* If the Customer changes the quantity of the Item to 0, the system deletes that Item from the Shopping Cart.

*Exceptional flow of events:* If the Customer presses the Delete button instead of the Update button, the system deletes that Item from the Shopping Cart.

*Exceptional flow of events:* If the Customer presses the Check Out button instead of the Continue Shopping button, the system passes control to the Check Out use case.

### Structure the Use Case Model

The team organizes the initial contents of the use case model for maximum efficiency. This can include using the includes and extends constructs and use case generalization, all of which are built into the UML; other constructs, such as precedes and invokes (see "Structure the Use Case Model" in Chapter 2), may also come into play.

# Analysis Activities

The following subsections describe the Analysis workflow activities that are of interest during the Elaboration phase.

### Perform Architectural Analysis

The architect partitions the system into analysis packages as part of the effort to expand the candidate architecture into an executable architectural baseline. The architect also seeks to identify generic mechanisms that will help the team perform analysis tasks, including collaborations that address things like error-handling, and packages such as those associated with the high-level view of how objects will be distributed. Also, the architect begins exploring ideas such as building a layered architecture.

The team building The Internet Bookstore decided before Iteration 2 that the analysis packages that they came up with during Inception (see Figure 7-3) were suitable going forward. During Iteration 2, the team decided to model a five-layer architecture. The layers, and their contents, were as follows:

- **Client**: the HTML pages that the Customer would use
- **Entity Beans**: the EJBs that would represent key classes from the domain model
- **Session Beans**: the EJBs that would implement the business logic and scheduling and such
- **Persistence**: classes that encapsulated access to persistent storage
- **System**: classes that encapsulated operating system features

See Scott Ambler's book *The Unified Process Elaboration Phase* (R&D Books, 2000) for more about this particular kind of architectural layering.

 **DELIVERABLE** The analysis model is a deliverable of each iteration within the Elaboration phase.

## Analyze a Use Case

The team generates use case realizations–analysis associated with all of the use cases being addressed within the given iteration. Each of the new use case realizations–analysis becomes part of the analysis model. The architect adds the architecturally significant use cases to the architecture description.

 **DELIVERABLE** The architecture description is a deliverable of each iteration within the Elaboration phase.

The team building The Internet Bookstore performed robustness analysis according to the schedule laid out during the Prioritize the Use Cases activity: Shopping Cart and Catalog use cases during Iteration 2; Account Management use cases during Iteration 3; and Order Processing, Inventory, and Accounting use cases during Iteration 4. Figure 8-3 shows the results of their analysis of the Edit Contents of Shopping Cart use case (Iteration 3).

While they were analyzing use cases during Iteration 2, the members of the team started mapping analysis objects to the architecture, as follows:

- The boundary objects went into the Client layer.
- The entity objects went into the Entity Beans layer.
- The control objects became candidates for inclusion in the Session Beans layer. (The team didn't make any commitments in this direction yet because it was too early to decide whether the control classes represented on the robustness diagrams should be "full" classes. Making these decisions is a key aspect of the Design a Class activity, which is discussed later in this chapter.)

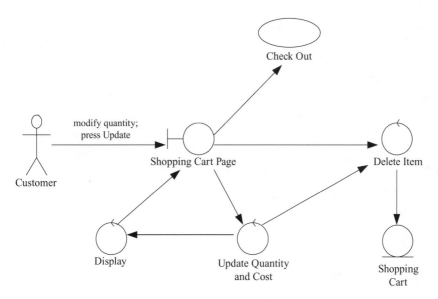

**Figure 8-3: Robustness Diagram for Edit Contents of Shopping Cart**

## Analyze a Class

The team expands the definitions of the analysis classes associated with all of the use case realizations–analysis being built within the given iteration. These become part of the analysis model. The architect adds the architecturally significant analysis classes to the architecture description.

The team building The Internet Bookstore defined analysis classes in parallel with their robustness analysis efforts. Figure 8-4 shows some of the analysis classes they had defined after Iteration 4.

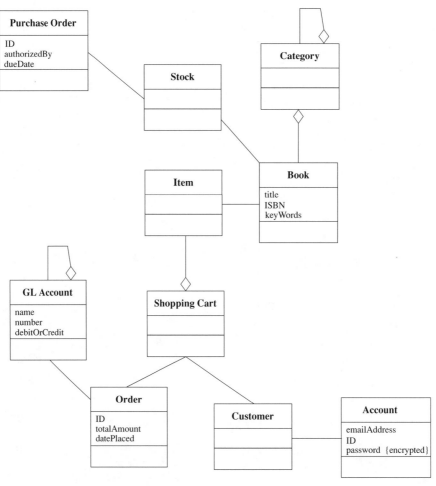

**Figure 8-4: Analysis-Level Class Diagram After Iteration 4**

Note the {encrypted} tagged value assigned to the *password* attribute within the Account class. This is indicative of the kind of detail that the team should feel free to start adding to attributes during analysis.

### Analyze a Package

The component engineers add the use case realizations–analysis and analysis classes associated with each current iteration to the analysis packages outlined by the architect. They may also break packages up, merge packages, or both, while ensuring that the integrity of the packages remains intact.

The team building The Internet Bookstore decided, during Iteration 3, that package Order Processing and Inventory needed to be broken into two packages. Figure 8-5 shows the effects of this change.

The figure shows that the Inventory package received the interfaces that were formerly part of the combined Order Processing/Inventory package, and that now the Order Processing package has dependencies on those interfaces.

## Design Activities

The following subsections describe the Design workflow activities that are of interest during the Elaboration phase.

### Perform Architectural Design

The architect does significant expansion of the deployment model and the design model from the versions done during the Inception phase. (See "Perform Architectural Design" in Chapter 4 for details.)

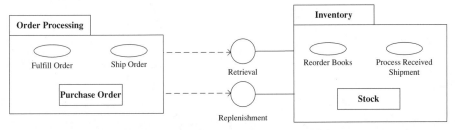

**Figure 8-5: New Analysis Packages After Iteration 3**

> **DELIVERABLE**    The deployment and design models are deliverables of each iteration within the Elaboration phase.

Figure 8-6 is one of the deployment diagrams that the team building The Internet Bookstore drew after Iteration 2. Note its use of user-defined stereotypes, which make it very clear which kinds of objects and communications protocols are in use.

Figure 8-7 shows some of the design-level classes relevant to the Shopping Cart package.

## Design a Use Case

The team generates use case realizations–design associated with all of the use cases being addressed within the given iteration. Each of the new use case realizations–design became part of the design model.

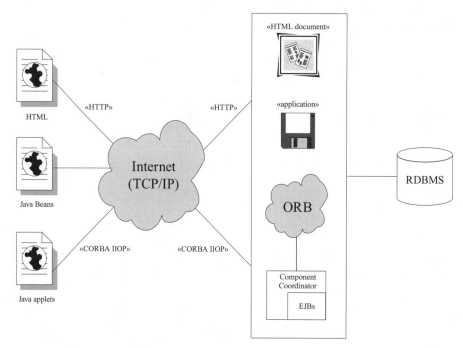

**Figure 8-6: Excerpt from Deployment Model After Iteration 2**

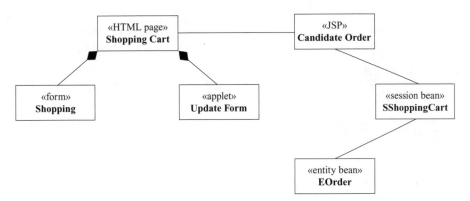

**Figure 8-7: High-Level Excerpt from Design Model After Iteration 2**

> **DELIVERABLE** The design model is a deliverable of each iteration within the Elaboration phase.

The architect adds the architecturally significant realizations to the architecture description.

Figure 8-8 shows the results of their initial design of the Edit Contents of Shopping Cart use case, which happened during Iteration 3.

Figure 8-9 shows the dynamic behavior of a design pattern that underlies the use case realization–design shown in Figure 8-3 as well as a number of comparable realizations that the bookstore team designed. The diagram shows how a client invokes an operation on an entity bean (a kind of EJB), as well as how a Bean Manager stores the result(s) of the operation in the database and then "passivates" the bean (puts it in a Pooled state, as opposed to the Ready state the bean was in when the operation call came in) when the operation has finished executing. Note that all the objects between the Client and the Database belong to a generic EJB container.

## Design a Class

The team expands the definitions of the design classes associated with all of the use case realizations–design being built within the given iteration. These become part of the design model.

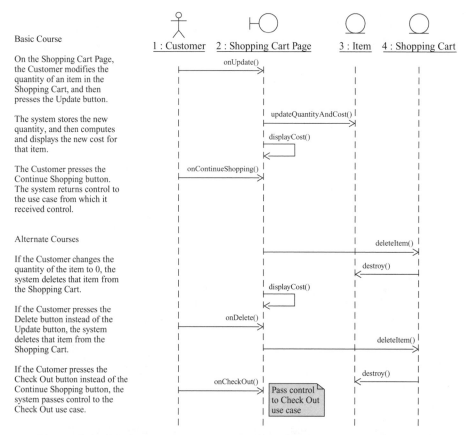

**Figure 8-8: Sequence Diagram for Edit Contents of Shopping Cart**

The team building The Internet Bookstore started defining entity beans and session beans for the use cases it was addressing during each Elaboration iteration. Figure 8-10 shows the classes that the team designed to comprise what will become the Shopping Cart Bean during the Implement a Class activity (described later in this chapter).

## Design a Subsystem

A component engineer designs a subsystem that contains some or all of the use case realizations–design and design classes relevant for the current iteration. The resulting design subsystem becomes part of the architecture description.

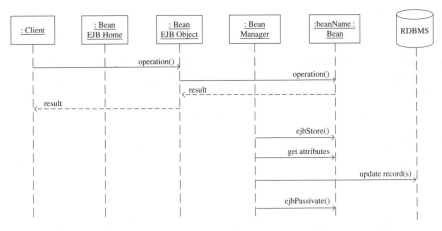

**Figure 8-9: Sequence Diagram for Operation Invocation on Entity Bean**

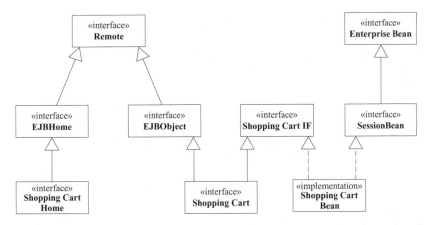

**Figure 8-10: Low-Level Excerpt from Design Model After Iteration 2**

The team building The Internet Bookstore defined and expanded upon design subsystems as they were defining use case realizations–design and design classes during all three iterations within Elaboration.

## Implementation Activities

The following subsections describe the Implementation workflow activities that are of interest during the Elaboration phase.

### Perform Architectural Implementation

The architect identifies which components the current iteration will require to implement the design subsystems, and then maps these components to nodes. This mapping is the basis of the implementation model; it also becomes part of the architecture description.

 **DELIVERABLE**    The implementation model is a deliverable of each iteration within the Elaboration phase.

As part of Iteration 2, the team building The Internet Bookstore defined a number of components in outline form. Seven of them, all of which the team defined as Java servlets, were designated to "live" on the Web server:

- **Book Details** retrieved the information, such as the thumbnail of the cover, the current price, and the various reviews that appeared when the Customer wanted to see the details about a particular book.

- **Book Base** contained a cached list of all available Books; other servlets called this one when they needed to retrieve information about particular Books.

- **Catalog** returned the results of Customer search and browse requests.

- **Login** handled Customer logins.

- **Main Page** was the first page a Customer saw when he or she got to The Internet Bookstore's site.

- **Purchasing** handled the conversion of a Shopping Cart to an Order and also interacted with the external financial entities that approved or denied Customer credit cards.

- **Shopping Cart View** handled Customer modifications to the contents of Shopping Carts.

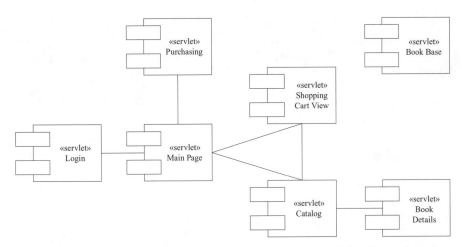

**Figure 8-11: Component Diagram for Web Server After Iteration 4**

Figure 8-11 shows the structural relationships among the components on the Web server.

Another seven of them were designated to "live" on the application server:

- **Book** was an entity bean that contained a Book's ISBN number, name, and author; a brief description; and the list price.

- **Cart Line Item** was a stateful session bean that contained a pointer to a particular Book in a Shopping Cart, the desired quantity of that Book, and the discount on the list price of that Book, as applicable.

- **Customer** was a stateful session bean that contained the key information necessary to log a Customer in and ship Orders to him or her.

- **Order** was an entity bean that contained information such as the total cost of an Order and the date it was placed; a Shopping Cart became an Order when the Customer gave final approval.

- **Order Line Item** was an entity bean that contained the same information as the associated Cart Line Item.

- **Pricer** was a stateless session bean that calculated the cost for each Cart Line Item in a Customer's Shopping Cart, based on list prices, discounts, and quantities.

- **Shopping Cart** was a stateful session bean that contained pointers to the Books that the Customer wanted to buy.

Note that the team defined some of the session beans described earlier as stateful, rather than stateless, to provide for the ability of a Customer to retrieve the contents of his or her Shopping Cart even after an interruption in the session.

Figure 8-12 shows the structural relationships among the components on the application server.

## Implement a Class

The component engineers build components that implement the design classes relevant to the current iteration. These components become part of the implementation model.

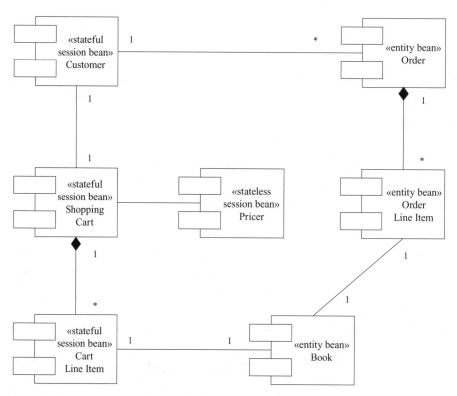

**Figure 8-12: Component Diagram for Application Server After Iteration 4**

The team building The Internet Bookstore built the components needed to implement the Shopping Cart use cases (Add Book to Shopping Cart, Check Out, and Modify Contents of Shopping Cart) and Catalog use cases (Search by Author, Search by Category, and Search by Title) during Iteration 4. These components included the Shopping Cart View and Catalog servlets (see Figure 8-11) and the Shopping Cart and Book EJBs (see Figure 8-12). The Shopping Cart session bean included methods to perform the following tasks, among others:

- Get the number of Books in the cart.
- Add a Book to the cart.
- Get the ID of the Customer to whom the cart belongs.

## Perform Unit Test

The component engineers perform black-box and white-box testing on the components for which they're responsible. The inputs and outputs of unit testing become part of the test model.

 **DELIVERABLE** The test model is a deliverable of each iteration within the Elaboration phase.

The team building The Internet Bookstore performed unit testing on the components they built during the Implement a Class activity. The unit testing on the Login servlet included tests of what would happen under the following conditions:

- The Customer provided a user ID that the system recognized and the correct password.
- The Customer clicked the New Account button instead of providing a user ID and password.
- The Customer clicked the Reminder Word button before providing a user ID and password.
- The Customer provided a user ID that the system didn't recognize.
- The Customer provided a password that didn't match up with the user ID that he or she provided.
- The Customer entered a bad password three times in succession.

Note the direct correlation between these conditions and the text of the Log In use case (see "Detail a Use Case" in Chapter 2).

### Implement a Subsystem

A component engineer builds a subsystem that contains some or all of the components produced during the Implement a Class activity. This subsystem becomes part of the implementation model.

The team building The Internet Bookstore built subsystems for the Web server and the application server. Each subsystem contained the components identified during the Perform Architectural Implementation activity, with those components that the team hadn't built yet represented as stubs.

### Integrate the System

The system integrator puts together an integration build plan for the builds to be done as part of the current iteration, and then integrates the necessary subsystems for each build into the executable architectural baseline.

The team building The Internet Bookstore integrated the partially implemented Shopping Cart and Catalog subsystems during Iteration 4. This integration enabled any user to perform the various searches on the book catalog, look at the details of any book, and add to and modify the contents of his or her shopping cart. (A user would also be able to "check out," but that option existed only as an abstraction, since the team hadn't built the mechanisms for checking the user's credit card or recording the order.) The integrated system became the first architectural baseline.

## Test Activities

The following subsections describe the Test workflow activities that are of interest during the Elaboration phase.

### Plan Test

The test engineer plans tests that the team can use to evaluate the architectural baseline. The test plan goes into the test model.

The team building The Internet Bookstore decided to focus its testing efforts on feature sufficiency (see "Plan Test" in Chapter 6). Within Elaboration, this included planning tests to be executed during Iteration 4 that measured how well the Shopping Cart and Catalog areas of the system worked together in terms of data flow and performance (for example, how quickly the system retrieved the names of all books written by Russ Coleman).

## Design Test

The test engineers design integration, system, and regression test cases, and associated test procedures that involve the architecturally significant use cases within the use case model. These test cases and test procedures go into the test model.

Since the first working version of The Internet Bookstore offered only Shopping Cart and Catalog functionality, the scope of testing across components was relatively small during Iteration 4. The tests that the team designed included the following:

- Tests involving catalog searches that would return result sets both small and large, and also searches guaranteed to produce no results
- Tests involving situations where the system had to make decisions about the price of a book (see the description of the Pricer bean in "Perform Architectural Implementation" earlier in this chapter) based on the presence of more than one available discount

## Implement Test

The test engineers build test components, as applicable, for integration and system testing. These test components go into the test model.

The team building The Internet Bookstore put together several test components to exercise the various interfaces to the Web server and application server components they implemented earlier in Iteration 4. The components aligned with this order of execution for integration testing:

- Clients (Web browsers) and stubs for the servers
- The Web server and a stub for the client
- The application server and a stub for the client

- Clients and the Web server
- Clients, the Web server, and the application server

### Perform Integration Test

Integration testers perform integration testing in order to test the viability of combinations of the pieces that comprise the architectural baseline.

The team building The Internet Bookstore performed integration testing during Iteration 4. This testing, which involved clients and the Shopping Cart and Catalog functionality the team had built into the Web server and the application server, followed the pattern described in the previous section.

### Perform System Test

System testers perform system testing in order to test the viability of the architectural baseline as a whole.

Integration testing for The Internet Bookstore covered all of the possible execution options for the version of the system created during Integration 4, so it served the purpose of system testing as well.

### Evaluate Test

The test engineers evaluate the results of integration and system testing (including the results of regression testing) and determine how to proceed. This will generally include updating the test model.

The team building The Internet Bookstore discovered some performance issues related to searching the catalog by title. They addressed these issues along the way during Iteration 4.

## Taking Stock

The following subsections describe what the team should do at the end of each iteration within the Elaboration phase and at the end of the entire phase.

## Assess Each Iteration

The focus of assessment of each Elaboration iteration should be the architecture. Each of the models represented within the architecture description should evolve in significant ways during each iteration. If this turns out to not have been the case for a given iteration, the project manager needs to make adjustments such as shifting work to subsequent iterations or scaling back the number of features that the team is exploring.

## Assess the Phase as a Whole

Here are some key questions to ask at the end of the Elaboration phase before work on the project proceeds:

- Do all the stakeholders agree on the basic direction of the project?
- Does everyone understand and agree upon the detailed requirements?
- Is there a solid executable architectural baseline that can evolve as requirements are explored and features are added?
- Have the significant risks been identified, and are plans in place for addressing them?
- Does it still make economic and business sense to proceed with the project?

If the answers to these questions are positive in the eyes of at least the majority of stakeholders, then the project should proceed into Construction. If not, then it's probably best to fold up the tent.

# Looking Ahead

The following subsections describe the tasks that the project manager should perform before the project proceeds to Construction.

## Make the Full Business Case

By the time the project reaches the end of the Elaboration phase, the development team should have a firm handle on its ability to bring the project in within the agreed-upon schedule, resource, and cost limits. It should also be fairly clear that the resulting system will provide the kind of economic value that the initial business case specified. At this point, then, the project manager refines and expands that initial version into a full business case.

 The full version of the business case is a deliverable of the Elaboration phase.

## Do Initial Planning for the Construction Phase

The project manager needs to establish some high-level objectives for Construction at this point, including

- Specify how the team will address the risks that could possibly threaten the success of the project.
- Complete all models, the architecture, and the architecture description.
- Build at least one version of the system that the team can deliver to the customers.
- Determine how many iterations the team should make during Construction.
- Estimate budget, schedule, and staffing requirements based on current knowledge and educated guesses.

The next chapter discusses planning for Construction in more detail.

# Chapter 9

# The Construction Phase

## Introduction

The primary goal of the **Construction phase** is to build a working version of the system that's suitable for delivery to beta customers, while continuing to mitigate risks that might threaten that delivery. The key steps involved in reaching this goal include:

- Finish the use case model. (This signifies that all of the functional requirements are agreed upon and addressed within the system.)
- Finish all of the other models: analysis, design, deployment, implementation, and test.
- Modify the architecture as necessary to ensure that the deliverable system reflects the intent specified by the architecture description.
- Monitor critical risks (the ones that threaten the viability of the system) and significant risks (the ones that may cause disruptions to budget, schedule, or both) and mitigate them as they materialize.

The following list offers an overview of how the five workflows (see Chapters 2 through 6) cut across the Construction phase.

- **Requirements**: During Construction, the team creates use cases that capture the remaining functional requirements.

- **Analysis**: The team adds elements to the analysis model in response to the new use cases.

- **Design**: The team adds elements to the design model and the deployment model as exploration of the new use cases proceeds.

- **Implementation**: This workflow is where most of the team's efforts will be concentrated during Construction. The result of this workflow is a working system that reflects all of the functionality that the stakeholders have agreed belongs in the system.

 An executable version of the system is a deliverable of the Construction phase.

- **Test**: Most of the integration and system testing occurs during Construction, in response to the various pieces of the deliverable system coming together.

# Getting Started

The following subsections describe the tasks that the project manager should perform before the development team begins the activities specified by the five workflows.

## Plan the Construction Phase

The objective of this task is to update the project plan to include a detailed description of how work in this phase will proceed, and also to update and expand upon the more abstract description of how work would proceed through Transition. The detail for the phase should include specific budget and schedule numbers for each iteration. The rough phase plan for the proposed Transition phases should reflect first-cut guesses at the number of iterations and associated budget, schedule, and staffing numbers.

> **DELIVERABLE** An updated version of the project plan is a deliverable of the Construction phase.

## Establish the Evaluation Criteria

The key criteria that the project team needs to meet during Elaboration are straightforward: the system is sufficiently mature and stable to release one or more beta versions without exposing either the development team or the users to unacceptable risks, and the beta users can use the system, with the help of user documentation and training materials, without requiring significant assistance from the development team.

# Requirements Activities

The following subsections describe the Requirements workflow activities that are of interest during the Construction phase.

## Find Actors and Use Cases

The team discovers the remaining actors and use cases and captures them in the use case model.

>  The use case model is a deliverable of each iteration within the Construction phase.

The architect adds the architecturally significant use cases to the architecture description.

>  The architecture description is a deliverable of each iteration within the Construction phase.

The team building The Internet Bookstore discovered four use cases during Iteration 5:

- Track Recent Orders and Write Customer Review, both performed by the Customer actor
- Write Editorial Review and Approve Review, both performed by the Editor actor

The team added Track Recent Orders to the Shopping Cart package and the other three use cases to the Catalog package.

Figure 9-1 shows these new use cases.

There were no changes or additions to the use case model during Iteration 6.

## Prototype the User Interface

Within Construction, this activity focuses on designing the look and feel of those parts of the user interface that address the remaining use cases in the use case model.

The team building The Internet Bookstore expanded two prototypes during Iteration 5 to address the use cases Track Recent Orders (Shopping Cart package), Write Customer Review, Write Editorial Review, and Approve Review (all Catalog package), which became part of the use case model during their performance of the Find Actors and Use Cases activity (see the previous subsection). There were no changes or additions to the user interface during Iteration 6.

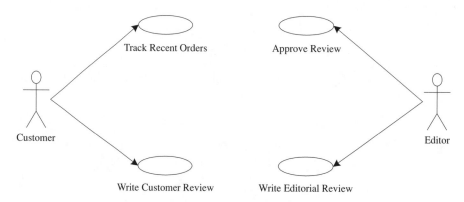

**Figure 9-1: New Use Cases After Iteration 5**

## Prioritize the Use Cases

The next task is to decide which of the remaining use cases to explore during which iteration within the Construction phase. This chunk of use cases should not represent more than 10 or 15 percent of the contents of the use case model.

The team building The Internet Bookstore made these decisions:

- **Iteration 5**: Design and build (implement) the Account Management use cases; build the Order Processing use cases; design the Inventory and Accounting use cases.
- **Iteration 6**: Build the Inventory and Accounting use cases.

## Detail a Use Case

The team writes detailed text, for the basic course and all alternate courses (see "Use Case" in Chapter 2), for all of the use cases being addressed within the given iteration.

The team building The Internet Bookstore wrote text for the use cases Track Recent Orders, Write Customer Review, Write Editorial Review, and Approve Review during Iteration 5. They didn't write any use case text during Iteration 6.

## Structure the Use Case Model

The team organizes the remaining contents of the use case model for maximum efficiency. This can include using the UML's include and extend constructs and use case generalization; other constructs, such as precedes and invokes (see "Structure the Use Case Model" in Chapter 2), may also come into play.

# Analysis Activities

The following subsections describe the Analysis workflow activities that are of interest during the Construction phase.

## Perform Architectural Analysis

The architect expands upon the analysis model that serves as the framework for analyzing the architecturally significant use cases and for designing and implementing generic mechanisms.

 The analysis model is a deliverable of each iteration within the Construction phase.

The team building The Internet Bookstore added the realizations of the use cases they started exploring during Iteration 5 to the analysis model. The model didn't require any more work during Iteration 6.

## Analyze a Use Case

The team generates use case realizations–analysis associated with all of the use cases being addressed within the given iteration. The architect adds the architecturally significant use case realizations–analysis to the architecture description.

The team building The Internet Bookstore performed robustness analysis on each use case it added during the Find Actors and Use Cases activity, more or less immediately after it became part of the use case model, during Iteration 5.

## Analyze a Class

The team expands the definitions of the analysis classes associated with all of the use case realizations–analysis being built within the given iteration. These become part of the analysis model. The architect adds the architecturally significant analysis classes to the architecture description.

The team building The Internet Bookstore added analysis classes to the analysis model in parallel with their robustness analysis work during Iteration 5. These classes included Order History (which participates in the realization of the Track Recent Orders use case) and Review, Customer Review, Editorial Review (all of which participate in the three new review-oriented use cases), with Customer Review and Editorial Review defined as subclasses of Review.

### Analyze a Package

The component engineers add the use case realizations–analysis and analysis classes associated with each current iteration to the analysis packages outlined by the architect, and ensure that the integrity of the packages remains intact.

The new use case realizations–analysis and analysis classes that The Internet Bookstore team worked with during Construction didn't affect the basic structure of the analysis model.

## Design Activities

The following subsections describe the Design workflow activities that are of interest during the Construction phase.

### Perform Architectural Design

The architect expands the deployment model and the design model as necessary to account for changes resulting from exploration of the implementation of the system.

 **DELIVERABLE** The deployment and design models are deliverables of each iteration within the Construction phase.

The team building The Internet Bookstore discovered that the architectural design work they performed during Elaboration resulted in an architecture robust and flexible enough that it didn't require any significant adjustments during either of the Construction iterations.

### Design a Use Case

The team generates use case realizations–design associated with all the use cases being addressed within the given iteration. The architect adds the architecturally significant realizations to the architecture description.

The team building The Internet Bookstore designed realizations for each use case it added during the Find Actors and Use Cases activity, more or less immediately after it became part of the use case model, during Iteration 5.

## Design a Class

The team defines design classes associated with all the use cases being addressed within the given iteration. The architect adds the architecturally significant design classes to the architecture description.

The team building The Internet Bookstore defined new classes for each use case it added during the Find Actors and Use Cases activity, more or less immediately after it became part of the use case model, during Iteration 5.

## Design a Subsystem

The team defines design subsystems associated with all the use cases being addressed within the given iteration. The architect adds the subsystems to the architecture description.

The team building The Internet Bookstore defined new subsystems, and refined and expanded existing subsystems, based on the use cases it added during the Find Actors and Use Cases activity, more or less immediately after they became part of the use case model, during Iteration 5. Figure 9-2 shows a high-level view, after Iteration 5, of a design subsystem they'd built and associated with the Account Management use case package.

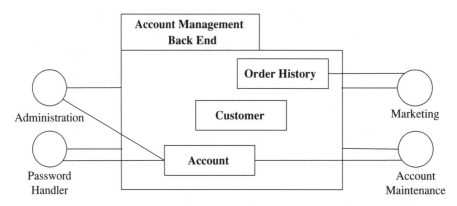

**Figure 9-2: Account Management Back End Design Subsystem**

## Implementation Activities

The following subsections describe the Implementation workflow activities that are of interest during the Construction phase.

### Implement a Class

The component engineers build components that implement the design classes that are relevant to the current iteration. These components became part of the implementation model.

 The implementation model is a deliverable of each iteration within the Construction phase.

The architect adds the components to the architecture description.

This is what happened with the team building The Internet Bookstore during this Construction activity:

- **Iteration 5**: The team built components associated with the Account Management use cases (Create Account, Log In, Modify Account, Suspend and Reactivate Account, and Update Customer History) and Order Processing use cases (Fulfill Order and Ship Order), including the Log In servlet (see Figure 8-11) and the Order EJB (see Figure 8-12).
- **Iteration 6**: The team built components associated with the Inventory use cases (Process Received Shipment and Reorder Books) and Accounting use cases (Post to GL, Print GL Report, and Set Up GL).

### Perform Unit Test

The component engineers perform black-box and white-box testing on the components for which they're responsible.

The team building The Internet Bookstore performed unit testing on the components they built during the Implement a Class activity.

### Implement a Subsystem

A component engineer builds a subsystem that contains some or all of the components produced during the Implement a Class activity.

The team building The Internet Bookstore completed the subsystems for the Web server and the application server and also built the subsystems for Account Management and Order Processing (during Iteration 5) and Inventory and Accounting (during Iteration 6). Each of the implemented subsystems followed the associated design subsystems fairly closely; see Figure 9-2 for an example of a design subsystem that the team put together.

### Integrate the System

The system integrator puts together an integration build plan for the builds to be done as part of the current iteration, and then integrates the necessary subsystems for each build into the executable architectural baseline. A given build may call for stubs for subsystems and components that haven't been built, but that elements of the current build depend on.

The team building The Internet Bookstore performed integrations during both iterations during Construction.

- During Iteration 5, users became able to log in and create and modify accounts, and the system became able to fulfill and record the shipment of orders.
- During Iteration 6, the system became able to reorder and stock books in inventory and to handle the back end accounting functions.

Each version of the integrated system became a new architectural baseline.

## Test Activities

The following subsections describe the Test workflow activities that are of interest during the Construction phase.

### Plan Test

The test engineer(s) plan tests that the team can use to evaluate each build of the system. The test plan goes into the test model.

> **DELIVERABLE**     The test model is a deliverable of each iteration within the Construction phase.

The team building The Internet Bookstore continued to focus on feature sufficiency (see "Plan Test" in Chapter 6) during Construction. The test plan for Iteration 5 was considerably expanded from where it stood for the last iteration in Elaboration, as the team now had to test the ability of the system to handle the complete life of an order, from user login (added via the Account Management system) through order fulfillment (as part of the Order Processing subsystem). Test planning during Iteration 6 focused on the ability of the system to handle out-of-stock conditions and credit card receipt processing.

## Design Test

The test engineers design integration, system, and regression test cases, and associated test procedures, that involve the remainder of the use cases within the use case model. These test cases and test procedures go into the test model.

The addition of the remaining functionality to The Internet Bookstore greatly expanded the scope of test design during Construction.

- During Iteration 5, the team focused on designing tests associated all of the things that could happen with a shopping cart and an order, including the Customer abandoning his or her cart before completing an order, and the system being unable to fulfil an order because a book associated with that order was out of stock. (The team had built a stub to stand in for the Inventory component until Iteration 6.)
- During Iteration 6, the team designed tests associated with the system's ability to respond more fully to out-of-stock conditions (which included reordering books) and to post accounting transactions, including receipts of credit card payments and payments to book suppliers, to the General Ledger.

## Implement Test

The test engineers build test components, as applicable, for integration and system testing. These test components go into the test model.

During Iteration 5, the team building The Internet Bookstore put together test components to exercise the new interfaces to the Web server and application server components that they implemented earlier in the iteration; during Iteration 6, they added test components to exercise the interfaces to the back end. The execution pattern was an expanded but similar version of the one described in the previous appearance of "Implement Test" (see Chapter 8).

### Perform Integration Test

Integration testers perform integration testing to test the viability of combinations of the pieces that comprise each build of the system.

The team building The Internet Bookstore performed integration testing during Iterations 5 and 6. Iteration 5 involved the servlets (on the Web server) and EJBs (on the app server) associated with Account Management and Order Processing, in addition to the elements that the team tested during Iteration 4. Iteration 6 added the back end Inventory and Accounting components to the integration testing task.

### Perform System Test

System testers perform system testing to test the viability of each build of the system as a whole.

The team building The Internet Bookstore had a number of users perform system testing by participating in various sequences of use cases that exercised all of the components of the system. One Iteration 5 sequence looked like this:

- Log In
- Search by Author
- Add Book to Shopping Cart
- Search by Author
- Add Book to Shopping Cart
- Modify Contents of Shopping Cart
- Check Out
- Fulfill Order
- Ship Order

## Evaluate Test

The test engineers evaluate the results of integration and system testing (including the results of regression testing) and determine how to proceed. This will generally include updating the test model.

The team building The Internet Bookstore found that it had to make two more passes through the Design Test activity to ensure an appropriate level of test coverage. (Once they finished that third pass, and the accompanying testing, they discovered that the system was, for all practical purposes, perfect, because they'd done such a good job with analysis and design.)

## Taking Stock

The following subsections describe what the team should do at the end of each iteration within the Construction phase and at the end of the entire phase.

### Assess Each Iteration

The focus of assessment of each Construction iteration should be the system as a whole. Each build of the system should represent a measurable improvement over the previous one. If this turns out not to have been the case for a given iteration, the project manager needs to make adjustments such as shifting work to subsequent iterations or scaling back the number of features that the team is building.

### Assess the Phase as a Whole

There's only one important question to ask at end of the Construction phase: Is the system ready to be delivered to beta customers? If not, then the phase really isn't over, and the project manager needs to add iterations or make other adjustments that will contribute toward the result of a deliverable system.

## Looking Ahead

The following subsections describe the tasks that the project manager should perform before the project proceeds to Transition.

### Update the Business Case

It's likely that the project manager will need to tweak the business case to some extent after Construction activities cease, based on the results of measuring budgeted values versus the actuals. The manager should be careful, though, to focus on the bigger picture, in terms of how the iterations went, as opposed to looking too closely at often-misleading metrics such as lines of code produced. If variances are relatively low, the business case shouldn't require much adjusting; however, if there are large variances in any key numbers, the project manager needs to set up sessions with the "outside" stakeholders within which some reassessment, and possibly significant reworking, of the business case happens.

 An updated version of the business case is a deliverable of the Construction phase.

### Do Initial Planning for the Transition Phase

The project manager needs to establish some high-level objectives for Transition at this point, including:

- Set up an environment in which chances are high that communication between the transition team and the customers will be strong.
- Complete beta versions of all documentation connected with the customers, including the requirements specification(s), user manuals, and training materials.
- Estimate budget, schedule, and staffing requirements based on current knowledge and educated guesses.

The next chapter discusses planning for Transition in more detail.

# Chapter 10

# The Transition Phase

## Introduction

The primary goal of the **Transition phase** is to deliver a working version of the system to the beta customers (and eventually the entire customer base), while successfully addressing defects that those customers uncover (as well as those concerns and desires for functionality that don't qualify as defects). The key steps involved in reaching this goal include the following:

- Preparing to roll out the system, which generally involves site preparation and advising the customer of necessary upgrades to hardware and system software
- Preparing documentation sufficient for the needs of beta customers
- Rolling out the system
- Tweaking the software as necessary to account for differences in customer environments (for instance, Netscape Communicator versus Microsoft Internet Explorer)
- Gathering information about defects and making corrections on a timely basis

The five workflows may come into play during Transition, but the Unified Process doesn't specifically address this subject. The assumption is that by the time the system reaches this point, it's demonstrably working.

## Getting Started

The following subsections describe the tasks that the project manager should perform before the development team begins the activities specified by the five workflows.

### Plan the Transition Phase

The objective of this task is to update the project plan to include a detailed description of how work in this phase will proceed. The detail for the phase should include specific budget and schedule numbers for each iteration.

### Establish the Evaluation Criteria

The key criteria that the project team need to meet during Transition are straightforward: the system has passed user acceptance testing; the accompanying documentation is accurate and useful; and the users are, in general, satisfied with the product.

## Activities

The following subsections describe the activities that the project team performs during the Transition phase.

### Get the Beta Release Out

The initial external release of the system should go to those customers who are likely to offer useful feedback on some or all aspects of the system. The focus should be on those customers who will be tough, but fair, critics because, after all, one doesn't learn as much from doing things right as from making mistakes. The delivery of the system should include whatever documentation the beta customers will need; ongoing customer support should, of course, be available to the greatest possible extent as well.

 The executable software is a deliverable of the
Transition phase.

## Install the Beta Release

Installing a beta release of the system usually involves customer-driven activity to some extent, unless the system is one that the project team (or associated personnel) can install for a relatively small set of internal customers. Sometimes this requires extensive instructions (and hand-holding over the phone, on-line, and via e-mail); other systems, such as The Internet Bookstore, require nothing more from (prospective) customers than that they point their browsers to the appropriate URL and start exploring. In any case, the project team needs to ensure that the beta customers understand how to report flaws in the system, whether in the form of formal acceptance testing or as something more informal.

 Installation software is a deliverable of the Transition
phase.

## Respond to Test Results

The results of user acceptance testing can be classified in one of two ways. Defects were discussed in Chapter 6; in this context, a defect is a bug in the system that interferes with its proper execution from the customers' standpoint. The project team deals with defects in the same manner as when it performed internal testing, except now it has to handle the ramifications of dealing with the customers who found the bugs. Beta testing may also uncover problems that are indicative of more serious flaws in the system; the team should handle these problems more formally, with options ranging from committing to address them in future iterations (or even cycles) to using a mechanism such as a change control board. In any case, the team should take extra care to ensure that changes to the system are reflected in the models and that they don't compromise the architecture.

## Adapt the Product to Varied User Environments

There are usually a number of variables associated with the environments in which the new system will be placed, including those related to the following factors:

- Internationalization, such as language, currency, laws and regulations, and politics
- Platform and other infrastructure
- The migration and conversion of data from existing systems and databases

The project team should make sure that it has addressed the relevant variables to the extent necessary to assure a reasonable level of acceptance of the system across the customer base. For instance, if the new system is replacing a legacy system, the team needs to work with the customers to determine what kind of cutover will produce the best result. The team also must deliver the appropriate legal documents, such as contracts, warranties, and license documents, to each customer site in parallel with delivery of the executable system.

 The set of legal documents associated with the system is a deliverable of the Transition phase.

## Complete the Artifacts

The project team should not consider the system deliverable until the important artifacts are reasonably complete. This includes:

- User and operator manuals, on-line help, and training materials

 User documentation and training materials are external deliverables of the Transition phase.

- The artifacts specifically described in Chapters 2 through 6, with emphasis on the six models and the architecture description

> **DELIVERABLE** The various models and the architecture description are internal deliverables of the Transition phase.

## Taking Stock

The following subsections describe what the team should do at the end of each iteration within the Transition phase and at the end of the entire phase.

### Assess Each Iteration

Generally, a team doesn't do more than one iteration within the Transition phase, but it may become necessary under some circumstances. For instance, if during the first iteration it became obvious that key requirements weren't addressed, or there's some significant technology-related failure, the project manager will need to call for at least a second iteration.

### Assess the Phase as a Whole

There's only one important question to ask at end of the Transition phase: Does the system work in the most typical user environments, and is customization work for atypical environments straightforward to perform? If not, then the phase really isn't over, and the project manager needs to add iterations or make other adjustments that will contribute to the result of a system with which the customers are satisfied.

## Looking Ahead

The following subsections describe the tasks that the project manager should perform before he or she considers Transition complete for the current cycle.

### Complete the Business Case

The project manager and the other stakeholders complete the business case for the project by completing the comparison of budgeted numbers versus actuals and capturing these and other metrics for use by future projects, and by evaluating the project's success level in terms of whether it attained the stated goals in terms of user satisfaction and economics.

## Do a Postmortem for the Project

The postmortem should address all the measurable aspects of the project, as well as the most important intangibles (such as those relating to the effectiveness of communication among the various stakeholders). The focus should be on issues such as potential reuse of project artifacts (from high-level use cases through the lowest-level chunks of code), training and mentoring, and the process itself.

## Plan the Next Release or Generation

Once the team reaches consensus that the current cycle is complete, there is likely to be strong sentiment to move forward toward the next cycle. The results of an effective postmortem should prove very helpful in creating the plan of attack for the next go-round.

# Appendix A

# The Rational Unified Process

The RUP is a specific and (highly) detailed instance of the Unified Process. Rational sells the RUP (see **http://www.rational.com/products/rup**) as a product that contains the following:

- An extensive set of HTML pages
- Tool mentors, which provide guidance for people working with the Rational Suite (a set of tools built around the RUP; the RUP is packaged with the Suite, but you can also buy the RUP separately)
- Templates for all of the major artifacts (for instance, Microsoft Word templates for things like the project plan)
- A set of manuals that describe things like how to configure the process template

The following sections describe the key aspects of what the RUP adds to the generic Unified Process framework.

## Workflows

The following subsections describe the nine workflows that the RUP defines.

## Project Management

The Project Management workflow contains those artifacts and activities related to project management that the Unified Process groups in with other workflows, and adds other relevant artifacts and activities. The artifacts include the risk list (as part of what the RUP calls the software development plan, or SDP), the business case, iteration plans, and a project measurements database; the activities include Plan for Next Iteration, Manage Iteration, and Close Out Phase.

## Business Modeling

The Business Modeling workflow contains the business model and domain model and the activities related to those models. It also breaks business rules out as a separate artifact and decomposes the business modeling activities that the Unified Process specifies into more finely grained activities.

## Requirements

The Requirements workflow is an expanded version of the workflow of the same name that the Unified Process defines, minus the material related to business modeling and domain modeling.

## Analysis and Design

The Analysis and Design workflow is a combination of the Analysis and Design workflows from the Unified Process, with additional artifacts and activities associated with modeling real-time systems.

## Implementation

The Implementation workflow is an expanded version of the workflow of the same name within the Unified Process.

## Test

The Test workflow is an expanded version of the workflow of the same name within the Unified Process.

## Configuration and Change Management

The Configuration and Change Management (CCM) workflow addresses the need to track and maintain the integrity of the various assets associated with a project. The central concept of this workflow is the CCM Cube, which contains the following visible faces:

- **Change Management**, which involves version control of the assets that comprise the product that the team is building
- **Change Request Management**, which involves formally managing requests for changes to the system that come in from stakeholders
- **Status and Measurement**, which involves tracking progress and measuring the results of activities

## Environment

The Environment workflow addresses the configuration and improvement of the software develoment process and associated tools, training, and technical services.

## Deployment

The Deployment workflow provides formal definitions of those activities that the project team performs during the Transition phase.

# Artifact Sets

The RUP defines five distinct sets of project artifacts.

- The **Management set** contains artifacts related to planning (the project plan, the iteration plans) and operation (status assessments, defect reports).
- The **Requirements set** contains the vision document, the use case model (and any associated documentation), and the business model.
- The **Design set** contains the design model, the architecture description, and the test model.

- The **Implementation set** contains the source code, the elements of the executable software, and any other necessary supporting data and files.
- The **Deployment set** contains the nonexecutable deliverables of the system, including installation material, user documentation, and training material.

## Workers

The RUP defines roughly twice as many workers as the Unified Process does. RUP workers include:

- **Toolsmith**, who's responsible for selecting and acquiring tools and providing ongoing support to users of the tools.
- **Process Engineer**, who's responsible for the software development process itself, which involves process configuration, measurement, and efforts to achieve continuous improvement.
- **Database Designer**, who's responsible for the logical and physical schema of the databases.
- **Technical Writer**, who's responsible for user documentation and, perhaps, training material. (Contact me at kendall@softdocwiz.com to learn about the *other* ways that good tech writers can add value to a project.)

# Appendix B

# Extreme Programming and the RUP

Kent Beck, in *Extreme Programming Explained: Embrace Change* (Addison-Wesley, 2000), defines XP as "a lightweight methodology for small-to-medium-sized teams developing software in the face of vague or rapidly changing requirements." All things considered, one wouldn't jump to the conclusion that XP has much to do with the Unified Process or the RUP, but there have been a lot of conversations, at conferences and in Internet forums, about the possibility that XP is an instance of the RUP. Let's take a look.

## A High-Level View of XP

At the conceptual center of XP are four values, five fundamental principles, and four kinds of development activities.

### Values

**Communication**—in particular, open and honest communication—is essential to virtually all of what goes on in the context of an XP project. As Beck says, "Problems with projects can invariably be traced back to somebody not talking to somebody else about something important."

**Simplicity** is represented in XP terms by the quest for "the simplest thing that could possibly work." The idea is to build something simple and straightforward that solves today's problem(s), and make sure that it's flexible enough to refine and expand to solve tomorrow's problems, but don't worry about tomorrow's problems today.

**Feedback** refers to feedback loops that work in time frames both small (days, even minutes, with regard to unit testing) and large (weeks and months—but never years) in association with user acceptance testing and project planning and scheduling.

**Courage** is the value that gives XP practitioners permission to pursue high-risk, high-reward paths through development tasks. This often manifests itself in the form of developers building throwaway prototypes during their coding efforts.

The idea is that the values work together to reward both individual needs and the needs of the group. For example, the better the communication, the easier it will be to consistently do the simplest thing, and that in turn allows the team to be more courageous because the risk of breaking existing functionality is lower.

## Fundamental Principles

**Rapid feedback** is critical to XP, because it enables team members to make adjustments quickly rather than let the effects of problems linger. This principle applies to both human feedback and the feedback connected with testing. (A secondary principle that goes along with this is "honest measurement," the premise of which is that the metrics to be applied to a project should correlate with how the project will go: not too coarse, not too fine.)

**Assume simplicity** corresponds with the value of simplicity described in the previous subsection. This principle dictates that the team should assume that every problem has a reasonably simple solution. This principle has the effect that the time saved on the majority of problems for which this turns out to be true frees up more time to attack those problems that really do require complex solutions.

**Incremental change** refers to both an overarching premise of an XP project—change the design a little, change the plan a little, change the code a little, because changing too much at once is a recipe for disaster—and also the way an organization should go about adopting XP (a little at a time).

**Embracing change** addresses the basic assumption that an XP project makes about requirements: They're uncertain more or less the whole time. The premise is that the members of the team should simply address change as a driving force on an everyday basis, rather than something that crops up occasionally. As Beck says at the end of his book, "By giving up explicit preparation for change, paradoxically [XP developers] become entirely prepared for any change."

**Quality work** is a stake in the ground with regard to the triangle represented by the various versions of the following: "Fast. Cheap. Good. Pick two." XP says, in effect, that if you're not going to something well, don't do it at all, regardless of what the schedule and the budget constraints might be.

XP also has a number of "secondary" principles, including **small initial investment** (start small in order to retain focus and reduce financial risk), **concrete experiments** (test abstract decisions, rather than relying on them going forward), and **accepted responsibility** (volunteer; don't wait to be asked).

## Development Practices

**Coding**, of course, refers to producing the one indispensable artifact of a software system. XP practitioners like to use code as a vehicle toward reaching several goals, including quick learning and improved communication. Several of XP's related practices tie directly to coding, including these:

- **Refactoring** is the craft of improving a system by restructuring program code without changing its behavior.
- **Pair programming** is the preferred practice of XP developers working in pairs at one computer.
- **Continuous integration** involves integrating and building a working version of the system every time the team completes a task—as often as several times a day.

**Testing** is inextricably linked to coding in the world of XP. One of the inviolable tenets of the methodology is that a developer shall write unit tests before writing code, and that developer shall demonstrate that his or her code passes all of these tests before that code gets to become part of the system. XP also places strong emphasis on functional tests, written at least in part by the customers, which are meant to demonstrate that the system meets their functional requirements.

**Listening** refers to ways to structure communication such that conversations, wherever possible, involve today's problems (not tomorrow's) and an appropriate level of detail. The ideal situation in the world of XP involves a customer who's available, for all practical purposes, all the time, and developers who have refined the art of listening to the point where it's easy to "cut to the chase" with that customer.

**Designing** refers to the need to create a structure that organizes the logic within the system in ways that make the system robust and maintainable. Another area of practice within XP is termed "simple design," which is in keeping with the value of simplicity described earlier in this appendix. Another phrase that captures the essence of what XP developers are after is "once and only once," which specifies that the system must communicate everything it needs to without any duplicate code (or, by extension, duplicate design elements).

On the project management side is another important aspect of XP called The Planning Game. This involves business people making decisions about things like scope and what should go in what release of the system, and technical people coming up with estimates and schedule details, in the context of a game whose phases are as follows:

- **Exploration** involves finding out what new things the system might be able to do.
- **Commitment** involves deciding what requirements to try and satisfy next.
- **Steer** involves guiding development by making ongoing adjustments to the plan.

The idea is that if each side stays focused on what it does best and plays by the rules of the game, a project has a much greater chance of success than if the stakeholders stray.

## XP and the RUP: Common Ground

On the one hand, it's fairly easy to see a number of areas where the XP and the RUP share ideas and practices.

- Both XP and the RUP emphasize the importance of facilitating communication among the various stakeholders in a project, although the RUP uses the UML explicitly toward that end, whereas XPers don't usually do formal modeling.

- Both XP and the RUP advocate continuous integration, albeit on different scales. Even though there are differences in the order in which things should happen, these processes share the idea of "analyze a little, design a little, code a little, test a little."

- Both XP and the RUP aim for simplicity, when you get right down to it. Where XP makes simplicity a core value and adds other guiding principles that dictate how to achieve it, the RUP also advocates that the team strive for use cases, architecture, and models that are easy for the people they affect to understand. (I hope you agree that this book supports this conclusion.)

## XP and the RUP: Key Differences

On the other hand, there are clearly some radical differences between the approaches of XP and the RUP to software development.

- The RUP represents what's fundamentally a top-down approach to a system, as indicated by its focus on starting with a skeletal architecture and fleshing out the "bones" with "meat" as development proceeds. XP is much more of a bottom-up approach; the clearest indication of this is XPers' tendency to "discover" the design in response to coding and ongoing refactoring of code. (Another sign is the fact that XP advocates like to speak in terms of "metaphor" rather than "architecture," which also offers some insight into some of the rather mystical aspects of XP that are beyond the scope of this appendix.)

- I mentioned earlier that XP advocates don't really believe in formal modeling. In practice, they don't believe in written documentation, period, outside of "user stories," their version of use cases. It's certainly the case that the RUP offers the opportunity for a team to avoid producing some, even many, artifacts for a given project, but the XP way is to rely on oral documentation as heavily as is feasible.

- As indicated at the beginning of this appendix, XP was conceived for use by small to medium-sized teams. The theoretical limit on team size is an open question at this point, but it's generally agreed that 10 or 12 developers is about as many as an XP project can handle. The need to have all of the developers in the same room, combined with the highly desirable situation wherein a customer is always available, makes it hard to picture XP being able to scale to a project of significant size. The RUP was specifically conceived as being a process aimed at big projects, with all that entails.

## So, Is XP an Instance of the RUP or Not?

It's an interesting idea, but I think not. XP and the RUP come from vastly different mindsets, and the cultural differences between XPers and RUP advocates are just too great to justify the conclusion that XP represents a highly tailored version of the RUP.

# Appendix C

# The ICONIX Process

The ICONIX process, created by Doug Rosenberg, sits somewhere in between the RUP and XP. This process is use case driven, like the RUP, but without much of the overhead associated with the RUP. It's also relatively small and tight, like XP, but it keeps analysis and design as full players.

The ICONIX process also makes streamlined use of the UML while keeping a sharp focus on the traceability of requirements. One phrase that captures the intent of the process is "minimal yet sufficient," with the idea that it is minimalist compared to the RUP yet sufficient where XP is not. Further, the process stays true to Ivar Jacobson's original vision of what "use case driven" means, in that it results in concrete, specific, readily understandable use cases that a project team can actually use to drive the development effort. (In fact, this process has its roots in the Objectory process, as does the Unified Process.)

Figure C-1 shows the "big picture" for the ICONIX process. The picture has two parts to it: The top part is the **dynamic model**, which describes behavior, and the bottom part is the **static model**, which describes structure.

One starts a project using this process by building a **domain model** (see the bottom left of Figure C-1), which serves as a glossary of the main abstractions—in other words, the most important nouns that belong to the problem space (which might also be called the **problem domain**). The nouns that belong to the problem space are called **domain objects**; the domain model lays the domain objects out on one big UML class diagram.

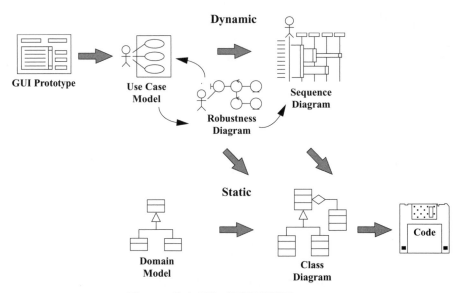

**Figure C-1: The ICONIX Process**

It's very useful to begin the exploration of the dynamic behavior to be built by doing some prototyping. This includes everything from simple line drawings of screens, windows, or HTML pages through fully working protoypes. Anything that will help the development team get some assurance from users that they're on the right track will be helpful.

Once the domain model and some prototypes are in place, the next step is to start defining use cases. The prototype material serves as an excellent source of use cases; the domain model provides the vocabulary that the team uses in writing the use case text. By doing the latter, the use cases describe system usage in the context of the object model, and thus contribute to use cases being very explicit, precise, and unambiguous.

The latter statement is at the heart of the stated purpose of the process: to produce use cases that people can actually use to drive system development through to code. As part of that effort, the team expands and refines the contents of the domain model—which is part of the static structure—as it learns more about the dynamic behavior.

The next step in the process is to perform robustness analysis (see "Use Case Realization–Analysis" in Chapter 3) on each use case. The robustness diagram sits in the gap between requirements (the "what") and detailed design (the "how"). A full set of these diagrams will help make getting from the use cases to the sequence diagrams easier by providing the following:

- A quick and easy way to ensure the completeness and correctness of the use cases
- The ability for the team to discover new objects (and thus classes), which enable continued expansion and refinement of the class diagrams at the heart of the static structure, and to make good decisions about fleshing out new and existing classes with attributes
- Checklists that help designers get off to good starts on their sequence diagrams

Robustness analysis sits at the conceptual center of the ICONIX process, because crossing the "what vs. how" gap is, almost invariably, a hard problem, and this technique enables practioners who use it rigorously to make the problem considerably easier to solve.

Once robustness diagrams exist for a set of use cases, detailed design can proceed. The process calls for the use of sequence diagrams as its primary detailed design technique. As was explained in Chapter 4, sequence diagrams show the messages that objects send to each other and, by extension, which object is responsible for each piece of functionality. Making these decisions about how to allocate behavior across objects is at the heart of detailed design.

The process specifies that a sequence diagram must be created for each use case. A designer can simply copy the boundary and entity objects from the associated robustness diagram onto the sequence diagram, and then allocate the behavior specified by the control objects (which the process calls **controllers**). In some cases, most of this behavior will end up on boundary objects and entity objects; in other cases, control objects on a robustness diagram will become actual objects. In any case, the evolution of the static structure continues as the designers add operations to the classes in response to this behavior allocation. It's the rich class diagrams that result, with full sets of attributes and operations, that form the static description of how the code will be organized.

The ICONIX process doesn't specifically address five UML diagrams—object diagram, collaboration diagram, state diagram, component diagram, and deployment diagram—but it also doesn't dictate that the development team shouldn't use them as appropriate (in other words, where they add value). For example, the state diagram is indispensable in designing real-time systems, whereas the component diagram can help the team visualize how the large chunks of a complicated system fit together. Since the process has a number of things in common with the Unified Process, the descriptions of these other UML diagrams in the main chapters of this book should offer insight as to where they'd come into play for a project using the ICONIX process.

See *Use Case Driven Object Modeling with UML* for a more detailed description of the ICONIX process, and *Applying Use Case Driven Object Modeling with UML: An Annotated E-Commerce Example* (Doug Rosenberg and Kendall Scott; Addison-Wesley, 2001) for a demonstration of how to apply the process in the context of building an E-commerce system.

# Bibliography

Scott Ambler: *The Unified Process Elaboration Phase*. R&D Books, 2000.

Len Bass, Paul Clements, and Rick Kazman: *Software Architecture in Practice*. Addison-Wesley, 1998.

Kent Beck: *Extreme Programming Explained: Embrace Change*. Addison-Wesley, 2000.

Robert Binder: *Testing Object-Oriented Systems: Models, Patterns, and Tools*. Addison-Wesley, 2000.

Martin Fowler with Kendall Scott: *UML Distilled*: *A Brief Guide to the Standard Object Modeling Language*, *Second Edition*. Addison-Wesley, 2000.

Erich Gamma, Richard Helm, Ralph Johnson, and John Vlissides: *Design Patterns: Elements of Reusable Object-Oriented Software*. Addison-Wesley, 1995.

Ivar Jacobson, Grady Booch, and James Rumbaugh: *The Unified Software Development Process*. Addison-Wesley, 1999.

Ivar Jacobson, Magnus Christerson, Patrick Jonsson, and Gunnar Overgaard: *Object-Oriented Software Engineering: A Use Case Driven Approach*. Addison-Wesley, 1992.

Ivar Jacobson, Maria Ericsson, and Agneta Jacobson: *The Object Advantage: Business Process Reengineering with Object Technology*. Addison-Wesley, 1995.

Philippe Kruchten: *The Rational Unified Process: An Introduction*, *Second Edition*. Addison-Wesley, 2000.

Dean Leffingwell and Don Widrig: *Managing Software Requirements: A Unified Approach*. Addison-Wesley, 2000.

Doug Rosenberg and Kendall Scott: *Applying Use Case Driven Object Modeling with UML: An Annotated e-Commerce Example*. Addison-Wesley, 2001.

Doug Rosenberg and Kendall Scott: *Use Case Driven Object Modeling with UML: A Practical Approach*. Addison-Wesley, 1999.

Walker Royce: *Software Project Management*: *A Unified Framework*. Addison-Wesley, 1998.

Kendall Scott: *UML Explained*. Addison-Wesley, 2001.

# Glossary

**active class** A class whose instances can own processes or threads.

**activity** A tangible unit of work with a well-defined responsibility that a *worker* performs.

**activity diagram** A UML diagram that shows the flows among the various activities that an object performs.

**actor** A role that a user can play with regard to a system; or an entity, such as another system or a database, that resides outside the system.

**alternate course of action** A path through a *use case* that represents an error condition or a path that the *actor* and the system take less frequently. Synonym: *exceptional flow of events*.

**analysis class** A class specified to the level of detail appropriate to the *Analysis workflow*, which generally means that an analysis class contains attributes but not operations.

**analysis-level class diagram** A *class diagram* whose primary contents are *analysis classes*.

**analysis model** A package of *analysis packages* that contains *use case realizations–analysis*, and associated *analysis classes*, that work together to realize the functionality specified by the *use cases* contained within the *use case model*.

**analysis package** A package that contains *analysis classes* and *use case realizations–analysis*. An analysis package can also contain other analysis packages.

**Analysis workflow** The set of *activities* aimed at building the *analysis model*.

**Analyze a Class** An *activity* that involves expanding the definition of an *analysis class* that participates in one or more *use case realizations–analysis*.

**Analyze a Package** An *activity* that involves building an *analysis package* that was defined during the *Perform Architectural Analysis* activity.

**Analyze a Use Case** An *activity* that involves building a *use case realization–analysis* for a *use case*.

**architect** A *worker* who is responsible for part or all of the *architecture* of the system being built.

**architectural baseline** The version of the *architecture* that contains expanded versions of the six models initialized during the *Inception phase*.

**Architectural risks** Risks associated with the ability of the *architecture* to serve as a strong foundation of the system and to be sufficiently resilient and adaptable to the addition of features in future releases of the system.

**architecture** The fundamental organization of the system as a whole. Aspects of an architecture include static elements, dynamic elements, how those elements work together, and the overall architectural style that guides the organization of the system. Architecture also addresses issues such as performance, scalability, reuse, and economic and technological constraints.

**architecture description** The collection of "architecturally significant" elements of the *use case model*, the *analysis model*, the *design model*, the *deployment model*, and the *implementation model*, plus any supplementary text.

**artifact** Any meaningful internal or deliverable chunk of information that plays a role in the development of the system, such as a model, a requirements document, or the business case.

**basic course of action** The sunny-day scenario of a *use case*, the main start-to-finish path that the *actor* and the system will follow under normal circumstances. Synonym: *main flow of events*.

**black-box testing** Testing that tries to verify the behavior of a given *component* without considering what's inside the component. Synonyms: *responsibility-based testing* and *specification testing*.

**boundary object** An object, represented in the *analysis model*, with which an *actor* associated with a *use case* interacts.

**build** An executable version of part of a system or an entire system.

**Build the Business Model** An *activity* that involves building a *business use case model* and a *business object model* so that the project team can understand the workings of the business they're modeling, in terms of internal workflows and external stimuli that influence the business's behaviors. This activity is defined within the *Requirements workflow*.

**Build the Domain Model** An *activity* that involves understanding and describing the most important classes that represent the problem space, as well as the relationships among those classes, at a fairly high level of abstraction. This activity is defined within the *Requirements workflow*.

**business actor** An *actor*, in the context of the *business use case model*, that describes a customer or a partner outside of the business being modeled.

**business entity** A conceptual thing (such as an account) or a concrete thing (such as a form) that participates in a *business use case*.

**business model** The combination of the *business object model* and the *business use case model*.

**business object model** A *model* that describes how *business use cases* are "realized" by set of workers using *business entities*.

**business use case** A *use case*, in the context of the *business use case model*, that describes a business process.

**business use case model** A *model* that contains *business use cases* and *business actors*.

**candidate architecture** An *architecture* made up of initial versions of the *use case model*, the *analysis model*, the *design model*, the *deployment model*, the *implementation model*, and the *test model*.

**candidate requirement** A suggested feature that may become a full requirement as development proceeds.

**class diagram** A UML diagram that shows classes and the relationships among them.

**class flow graph** A combination of *method flow graphs* that models all control flow paths through the class as a unit.

**collaboration** A collection of classes and other elements that work together to provide some behavior.

**collaboration diagram** A UML diagram that focuses on the organization of the objects that participate in a given set of messages.

**component** A physical and replaceable part of a system that conforms to, and realizes, a set of *interfaces*.

**component diagram** A UML diagram that shows a collection of related *components*.

**component engineer** A *worker* who, within various workflows, is responsible for the definitions of the various aspects of one or more *analysis classes* and the contents of one or more *analysis packages*; for the definitions of the various aspects of one or more *design classes* and the contents of one or more *design subsystems*; for the source code of one or more «file» *components* and the contents of one or more *implementation subsystems*; and for building one or more *test components*.

**conformance-directed testing** A kind of testing, the goals of which involve executing tests designed to establish conformance to customer requirements.

**Construction phase** The *phase* during which the development team tries to build a system capable of operating successfully in beta customer environments.

**control flow graph** A graph that shows which chunks of code can be followed by which other chunks.

**control object** An object represented in the *analysis model* that embodies application logic.

**cycle** A period of time within a development project that ends with the release of a version of the system to customers.

**defect** A problem with the system that developers need to track and resolve.

**deployment component** A *component* that represents an executable part of a system.

**deployment diagram** A UML diagram that shows a collection of *nodes* and the dependencies and associations among those nodes.

**deployment model** A *model* that defines the physical organization of the system in terms of computational *nodes*.

**Design a Class** An *activity* that involves expanding the definition of a *design class* that participates in one or more *use case realizations–design*.

**Design a Subsystem** An activity that involves designing a *design subsystem* that was defined during architectural design.

**Design a Use Case** An activity that involves building a *use case realization–design* for a *use case*.

**design class** A class specified to the level of detail appropriate to the *Design workflow*, which generally means that a design class contains a full set of attributes and operations and a richer set of details about things like visibility.

**design-level class diagram** A *class diagram* whose primary contents are *design class*es.

**design model** A *model* that contains *use case realizations–design*, as well as associated *design class*es, that realize the functionality specified by the *use case*s contained within the *use case model*, the *analysis model*, and the *supplementary requirements*.

**design subsystem** A UML *package* that contains *design classes*, class and subsystem *interfaces*, and *use case realizations–design*.

**Design Test** An *activity* that involves designing the various levels of tests that QA staff need to perform on each build of the evolving system, as well as the procedures they'll follow to carry out those tests.

**Design workflow** The set of activities aimed at building the *design model*.

**Detail a Use Case** An *activity* that involves writing text for the *basic course of action* and *alternate courses of action* for a *use case*.

**domain model** A *model* that captures the important real-world things and concepts that belong to the "problem space," which defines the problem that the new system is being built to solve, in the form of classes and the various kinds of relationships among them.

**Elaboration phase** The *phase* during which the development team tries to establish the ability to build the new system given the financial constraints, schedule constraints, and other kinds of constraints that the development project faces.

**entity object** An object represented in the *analysis model* that contains long-lived information, such as that associated with databases.

**Evaluate Test** An *activity* that involves evaluating the results of integration and system testing by comparing those results to the appropriate quality goals described in the test plan.

**exceptional flow of events** A path through a *use case* that represents an error condition or a path that the *actor* and the system take less frequently. Synonym: *alternate course of action*.

**execution component** A *component* created as a result of an executing system.

**extend** A relationship within which a base *use case* implicitly includes the behavior of another use case at one or more specified *extension points*.

**extension point** A point in a *use case* from which an *extend* relationship goes out to another use case.

**fault-directed testing** A kind of testing, the goals of which involve executing tests designed to have a high probability of revealing faults.

**feature list** A document that identifies and briefly describes suggestions that can be seen as *candidate requirements*.

**Find Actors and Use Cases** An *activity* that involves discovering the human and non-human *actors* that will be interacting with the system, and putting together a set of *use cases* that reflect the behavior those actors will be performing in conjunction with the system.

**flow of events** A path through a *use case*.

**framework** An architectural *pattern* that provides a template one can use to extend applications.

**glossary** A collection of the various terms, specific to the system, that are in use in the other project *artifacts*.

**grammatical inspection** A task that involves analyzing a document, such as a requirements document or functional specification, and circling or highlighting nouns that might become classes and verbs that might become associations between classes. Synonym: *noun-verb analysis*.

**Implement a Class** An activity that involves expanding the definition of a *design class* and building a «file» *component*, or expanding an existing «file» component, to contain the class, and generating code for the operations that the design class specifies and for the various relationships in which that class is involved.

**Implement a Subsystem** An *activity* that involves building an *implementation subsystem* that was defined during architectural implementation.

**implementation-based testing** Testing that tries to verify the internal workings of the code inside a method, class, or *component*. Synonyms: *structural testing* and *white-box testing*.

**implementation model** A *model* that contains *components* and *implementation subsystems* that realize the functionality specified by the *use cases* contained within the *use case model*, the contents of the *design model*, and the *supplementary requirements*.

**implementation subsystem** A package that contains *components* and *interfaces* connected to components and other implementation subsystems.

**Implementation workflow** The set of activities aimed at building the *implementation model*.

**Implement Test** An *activity* that involves creating *test components* that automate *test procedures* by using a test automation tool, programming the components, or both.

**Inception phase** The *phase* during which the development team tries to establish the case for the viability of the proposed system.

**include** A relationship within which one *use case* explicitly includes the behavior of another use case at a specified point within a *basic course of action* or an *alternate course of action*.

**increment** A release of the system that contains added or improved functionality over and above the previous release. An increment is the result of a completed iteration.

**Initial Operational Capability** The *major milestone* associated with the *Construction phase*.

**Integrate the System** An *activity* that involves creating or expanding the *integration build plan* so that it reflects the contents of the next *build* of the system, and integrating the various pieces of that build together before integration testing begins.

**integration build plan** A plan that describes the *builds* that will occur within an *iteration*.

**integration tester** A *worker* who is responsible for performing integration testing.

**interface** A collection of operations that represent services offered by a class, subsystem, or *component*.

**iteration** A mini-project that results in an *increment*.

**Life-Cycle Architecture** The *major milestone* associated with the *Elaboration phase*.

**Life-Cycle Objectives** The *major milestone* associated with the *Inception phase*.

**main flow of events** The sunny-day scenario of a *use case*, the main start-to-finish path that the *actor* and the system will follow under normal circumstances. Synonym: *basic course of action*.

**major milestone** A point at which managers make important decisions about whether to proceed with development, and, if so, what's required.

**method flow graph** A graph that shows how an object reaches various states in response to what's going on inside of a method execution.

**model** A simplification of reality that helps people understand the complexity inherent in software. A model represents a complete view of the system from some viewpoint.

**node** A piece of hardware that represents some kind of computational resource, which generally has memory and may have processing capability.

**noun-verb analysis** A task that involves analyzing a document, such as a requirements document or functional specification, and circling or highlighting nouns that might become classes and verbs that might become associations between classes. Synonym: *grammatical inspection*.

**package** A conceptual grouping of pieces of a *model*.

**pattern** A solution to a problem that's common to a variety of contexts.

**Perform Architectural Analysis** An *activity* that involves creating outlines of the *analysis model* and of the *architecture* as a whole.

**Perform Architectural Design** An *activity* that involves creating outlines of the *deployment model* and the *design model*.

**Perform Architectural Implementation** An *activity* that involves identifying architecturally significant *components* and mapping the associated executable components onto *nodes*.

**Perform Integration Test** An *activity* that involves performing manual and automated integration testing.

**Perform System Test** An *activity* that involves performing manual and automated system testing.

**Perform Unit Test** An *activity* that involves producing executable code from a «file» *component*, then performing specification tests and structural tests on that code independent of other components.

**phase** The span of time between two *major milestones*. The Unified Process defines four phases: the *Inception phase*, the *Elaboration phase*, the *Construction phase*, and the *Transition phase*.

**Plan Test** An *activity* that involves building the *test plan*, which describes the QA resources that will be available for testing and the schedule of tests, as well as the test strategy, which specifies what tests will be performed within each *iteration* and things like required levels of code coverage.

**Prioritize the Use Cases** An *activity* that involves assigning priorities, based on technical and nontechnical considerations, to the various *use cases*.

**Product Release** The *major milestone* associated with the *Transition phase*.

**Prototype the User Interface** An *activity* that involves building the user-interface prototypes.

**realization** The relationship between an *interface* and a class or *component* that provides the interface's operations, or between a *use case* and the *collaboration* that represents the implementation of that use case.

**realize** To provide a concrete representation of an abstract concept.

**Requirements risk** The risk of not building the right system—the system that the customers are paying for—by not understanding the requirements and not using associated *use cases t*o drive development.

**Requirements workflow** The set of activities aimed at building the *use case model*.

**responsibility-based testing** Testing that tries to verify the behavior of a given *component* without considering what's inside the component. Synonyms: *black-box testing* and *specification testing*.

**robustness analysis** A task that involves taking each sentence of a *use case*, determining the *boundary objects*, *entity objects*, and *control objects* that it needs in order to address the behavior it specifies, and drawing those objects and their relationships.

**robustness diagram** A special form of UML collaboration diagram that contains a *use case realization–analysis*.

**sequence diagram** A UML diagram that focuses on the time ordering of the messages that go back and forth between objects.

**service** An atomic (indivisible) chunk of functionality that appears in one or more *use cases*.

**service package** A special type of *analysis package* that models a *service*.

**service subsystem** A special type of *design subsystem* that models a *service*.

**specification testing** Testing that tries to verify the behavior of a given *component* without considering what's inside the component. Synonyms: *black-box testing* and *responsibility-based testing*.

**state diagram** See *statechart diagram*.

**statechart diagram** A UML diagram that shows the different states that an object can assume during its life, the transitions that can happen between those states, and the various kinds of events that the object can respond to, as well as the nature of those responses.

**structural testing** Testing that tries to verify the internal workings of the code inside a method, class, or *component*. Synonyms: *implementation-based testing* and *white-box testing*.

**Structure the Use Case Model** An *activity* that involves breaking up *use cases* in search of simpler ones.

**supplementary requirement** A nonfunctional requirement that deals with an issue such as performance, security, backup, or constraints imposed from outside the system, such as those involving regulatory agencies.

**system analyst** A *worker* who focuses on capturing the requirements related to the *use cases*.

**system integrator** A worker who is responsible for designing the *integration build plan* and performing incremental integration of *builds*.

**system tester** A *worker* who is responsible for performing system testing.

**Technical risks** Risks associated with the various technologies that will come into play during the project and with issues such as performance and the "-ilities" (reliability, scalability, and so forth).

**test case** A specification of how one should test part of a system, including the inputs, the expected outputs, and the conditions under which the test should occur.

**test component** A piece of code that automates all or parts of one or more *test procedures*.

**test engineer** A *worker* who is responsible for planning integration, system, and regression testing, selecting and describing *test cases* and corresponding *test procedures*, ensuring the completeness and consistency of the *test model*, and evaluating the results of testing.

**test evaluation** An evaluation of the results of a set of tests that generally includes a list of *defects* and their priority levels, as well as statistical information, such as the ratio of defects to lines of code.

**test model** A *package* that contains the *test cases*, *test procedures*, and *test components* for the system being built.

**test plan** A document that describes the QA resources that will be available for testing and the schedule of tests, as well as the test strategy, which specifies what tests will be performed within each iteration and details such as required levels of code coverage.

**test procedure** A specification of how to perform all or parts of one or more *test cases*.

**Test workflow** The set of activities aimed at building the *test model*.

**Transition phase** The *phase* during which the development team tries to roll out the fully functional system to its customers.

**use case** A sequence of actions that an *actor* performs within a system to achieve a particular goal.

**use case diagram** A UML diagram that shows *actors*, *use cases*, and the relationships among them.

**use case engineer** A *worker* who builds one or more *use case realizations–analysis* and one or more *use case realizations–design*.

**use case model** A *model* that captures the functional requirements of the system. This model allows the project stakeholders to agree on the capabilities of the system and the conditions to which it must conform.

**use case realization–analysis** A *collaboration* that describes how the *actor(s)* and the system perform a given *use case*, in terms of *analysis classes*.

**use case realization–design** A *collaboration* that describes how the *actor(s)* and the system perform a given *use case*, in terms of *design classes*.

**use case specifier** A *worker* who writes detailed descriptions of the *main flow of events* and *exceptional flows of events* for one or more *use cases*.

**user-interface designer** A *worker* who provides the visual shaping of the user-interface prototype that one or more *actors* will use.

**white-box testing** Testing that tries to verify the internal workings of the code inside a method, class, or *component*. Synonyms: *implementation-based testing* and *structural testing*.

**worker** A role played by an individual, or a group of individuals working together as a team, on a project.

**workflow** A set of *activities* that various project *worker*s perform. The Unified Process defines five core workflows: the *Requirements workflow*, the *Analysis workflow*, the *Design workflow*, the *Implementation workflow*, and the *Test workflow*.

**work product component** A *component* that is part of the system but is not executable.

**work unit** A set of *business entities*.

# Index

# Also Available from Addison-Wesley

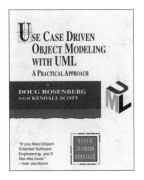

## Use Case Driven Object Modeling with UML
by Doug Rosenberg and Kendall Scott

0-201-43289-7 • ©1999 • Paperback • 192 pages

*Use Case Driven Object Modeling with UML* provides practical guidance that shows developers how to produce UML models with minimal startup time, while maintaining traceability from user requirements through detailed designing and coding. The authors present proven methods for driving the object modeling process forward in a straightforward manner.

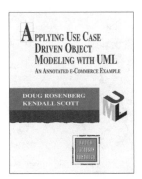

## Applying Use Case Driven Object Modeling with UML
*An Annotated e-Commerce Example*
by Doug Rosenberg and Kendall Scott

0-201-73039-1 • ©2001 • Paperback • 176 pages

This companion workbook to *Use Case Driven Object Modeling with UML* bridges the gap between the theory presented in the authors' first book, and the practical issues involved in the development of an Internet/e-Commerce application. Uniquely conceived as a workbook, featuring an e-Commerce system for an online bookstore as a running example, the book dissects its design in detail, demonstrates the most common design mistakes, and reveals the correct solutions.

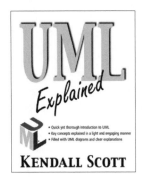

## UML Explained
by Kendall Scott

0-201-72182-1 • ©2001 • Paperback • 176 pages

Assuming no prior knowledge of the UML, object-oriented design, or programming fundamentals, this book fully explains basic concepts and terminology such as objects, classes, and use cases. It shows how the UML integrates with an iterative and incremental process.

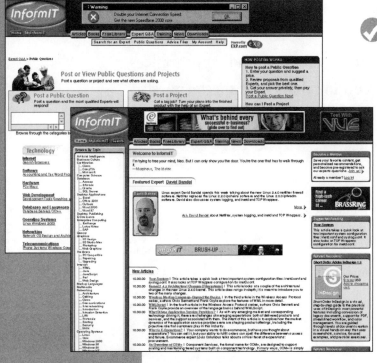